Rider-Shari Patterson,
Photographer-Mary Phelps

Rider- Liz Cline (author),
Photographer- Don O'Connor

"Here I am in my 5th Silver Medal winning ride with Liz Cline"
Photographer- Sheri Scott

Author- Liz Cline
Photographer- Reg Batt

Rider- Anne Patterson Chamberlain,
Photographer- Mary Phelps

Rider- Teri Hallman,
Photographer- J.D. Farrell

A Guide to HORSES
FROM THE HORSE'S MOUTH

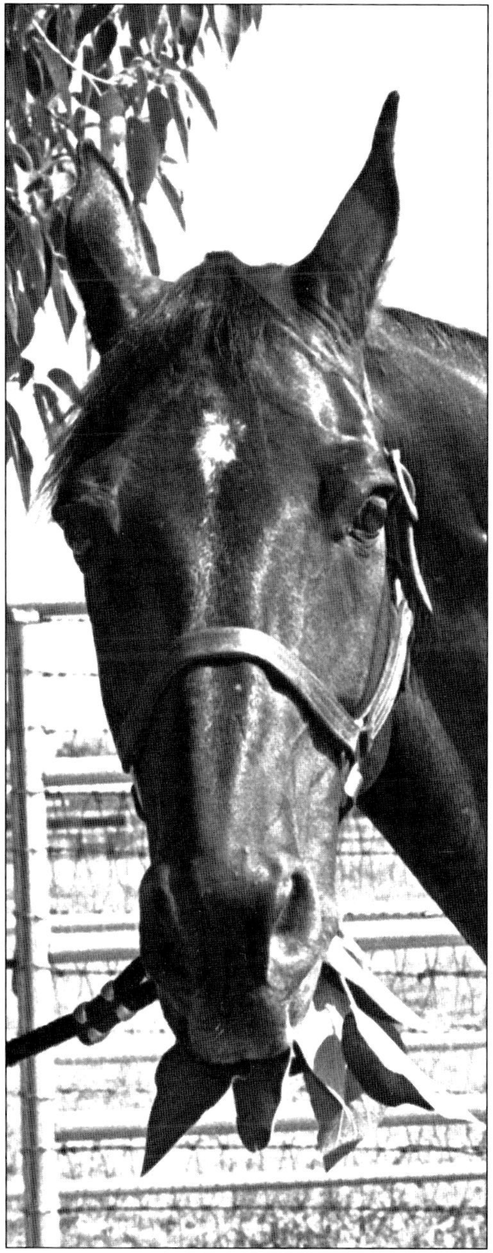

Champs the Schoolmaster

from the **Horse of Course Series**

Heartland Education

Dedicated to all children and their natural love of learning

Photo Credits — *All black and white photographs by Don O'Connor unless otherwise indicated. Cover photograph by Reg Batt and Herb Stokes of Portraits by Reg, Tempe, Arizona.*

Published by — Heartland Education Corporation
P.O. Box 61178
Phoenix, Arizona 85082-1178

Book Design — Shannon Bodie, Lightbourne Images, Ashland, OR

Library of Congress Catalog Card No. 96-94447
ISBN 0-9652995-4-6

Acknowledgements

A*s with any work of this type, there is never enough space to thank and acknowledge all who deserve recognition. However, there are those to whom I would be remiss if I failed to mention. Thus, I would like to thank my husband Jon, for all his love and understanding, and for all the very long nights of staying up and helping make this book what it is. Also to my mother, Lee Loney, for the endless miles she hauled my pony and horses, and the endless patience and understanding she had with my passion for horses. I must also thank Michael Hufnagel, D.V.M., Russell Brown, D.V.M. Assistant, Kirk Haspel, Farrier, Shari Patterson, Anne Patterson-Chamberlain, Jon Cline Jr., Lendy Cline, and Teri Hallman for being so accommodating as photo models. Others who must be mentioned for help with various aspects of this project include Curtis Vick, Gene Leafty, Montessori Teachers Margo O'Neal and Patty Langhurst, Shari Patterson, Karen Patterson, Susan Crocker, Tom Netting, Lloyd Benner, Attorney at Law, Ted Osowski, C.P.A., D. Scott Taylor, D.V.M., Photographers Don O'Connor, Reg Batt, and Herb Stokes, and my coach and mentor Shirley Rector. A special thank you also goes to Dan Donati in memoriam for collaborating with me years ago on this, and future works.*

About the Author

L*iz Cline's writing is informative, interesting and entertaining. She makes learning fun without losing the reader's attention in minor detail. This is born of her belief that children who develop a love of learning, and are motivated partly for the sheer joy of the exercise, are best equipped to deal with life's endeavors. With her own children in schools which foster this 'love of learning' concept, she believes that the comment "I made a 100% on my math test" is much less positive than "I can't wait to get to math class". One of her goals as an author is to help other children develop this attitude.*

As a child, she always considered herself to be one of the lucky ones. She had a horse as a friend and companion from the age of nine. Participation in activities and competition from 4H Club to Federation Equestre Internationale level Dressage, including multiple national titles and awards, has provided her with a wealth of experience and training in all aspects of horses. With a Baccalaureate degree in Equine Science and twenty years experience in private education, including ownership of a technical school in Phoenix, AZ, she has established an expertise exceeding knowledge of horses. She can also impart that knowledge to others.

Liz lives in Tempe, Arizona, with her husband Jon, children Jon, Jr. and Lendy (who are also involved in hockey, soccer, and baseball), and her three horses. While it is a given that one of these is Champs Elysees another is her original equine friend, Sonny, a 30+ year young pony.

Author's Note to the Reader

The vast majority of children have a strong attraction, if not an emotional love, for horses. Children who have horses often develop a bond as strong as that which they have with only their closest friends. Children who do not have a personal relationship with horses seem to long for one, often into adulthood. And with good reason. Horses can be kind and gentle giants who respond well to human requests. When well trained and free of bad habits, horses can represent the ultimate in freedom and speed to a child. They can also be the one friend a child can tell their deepest secrets to without fear of reprisal or ridicule.

This publication is intended to nurture this enchantment for horses through a greater entry level understanding of their proper care and maintenance. Further, to develop realistic expectations of how horses think, feel, and respond to people based upon factual knowledge. The intention is to help build confidence on the part of the beginner who can be intimidated by the sheer size difference between themselves and the horse. Also, there needs to be an awareness that horses can hurt people, so they must be treated with caution and respect.

This work has been a labor of love built upon years of education, experience, and training. Hopefully, the children of all ages who read this will have half as much fun with it as I had creating it.

How to Use This Book

This book is intended to be educational as well as entertaining. Upon completion, each child is eligible to receive a certificate and medal in honor of their accomplishment. ***To receive these awards,*** *follow the directions on the Completion Verification at the end of this book and return it to Heartland Education. Within 3 to 4 weeks, these awards will be delivered by courier or U.S. Mail.*

The author is dedicated to insuring the enjoyment by all readers of this work. All comments are welcome.

Table of Contents

Acknowledgements v

Note from the Author vi

Saddle Up! **1**

Food **11**

Health **23**

Shoeing **33**

Grooming **39**

Sleep and Rest **47**

Behavior **51**

Many Happy Trails to You! **61**

To Parents 65

Appendix 71

Index 73

Photo by Reg Batt and Herb Stokes

Saddle Up!

Get ready for an exciting trip which will help you learn about a very special animal; a horse. Horses are those gentle giants with big eyes and soft noses who have served people of all countries for hundreds of years. We want to know them, be close to them, and have them for friends.

This will be the first step in getting to know about these fine animals. More than that, the information comes straight from the horse's mouth.

You see, my horse Champs will be your teacher. Just as he has been my teacher and friend, he will speak to you on the topic he knows best, horses. Champs is well suited for this task. He is a very talented animal who is known as a Schoolmaster. That is, he is a horse whose job is teaching riders how to ride well. He is also very kind and gentle, so if a rider makes a mistake, he will usually not get frightened and cause the rider to get hurt.

In real life Champs has helped five ***riders***[1] *earn their USDF (United*

1 *Rider*: A person who rides a horse. In a horse show the rider can win awards when they ride their horse well.

States Dressage Federation) silver medals. Dressage is a type of riding and training; sort of like gymnastics, ballet, and figure skating call for a certain type of training. It is very hard for horses to do, and not many horses in the United States can say that five of their riders are silver medal winners.

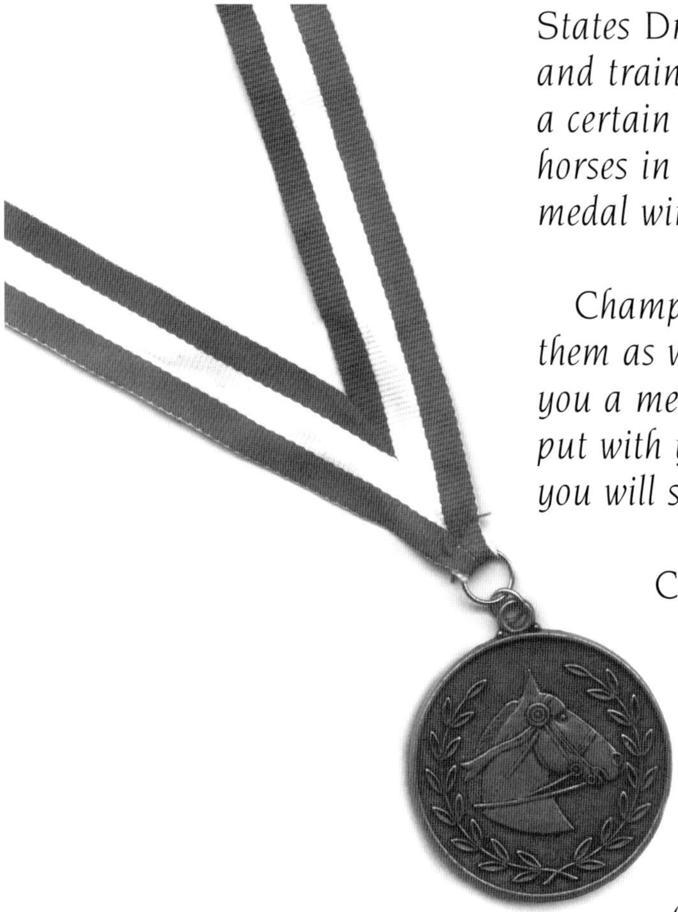

Champs has won many national awards and has helped his riders get them as well. When you have finished reading this book he will even send you a medal too. You will get the Horse Of Course Completion Medal to put with your other trophies. As you grow older and learn more, I believe you will still look back to this book by Champs for information.

Champs will help you learn that we are all caretakers of our animals. We need to put ourselves in their places and think the way they do. This will help us understand these friends who are entrusted to us.

Even though they cannot talk, they can teach us if we only let them. Please pay careful attention now as I leave you with my enchantingly graceful, loyal and honest friend, Champs Elysees.

24

Sheri Scott
95

Hello students, my name is Champs Elysees. There is a street in Paris, France, with the same name. When the French say this name it sounds something like **Shanz Elee say**, but my friends call me Shomps and I would like it if you would too.

I was born in Pinneberg, Germany, and I am a registered **Holsteiner**. Whoops, there is another funny word. When someone says this word, it sounds like Hole stine er. That means my type of horse comes from the Holstein area of Germany.

I was trained by a German ***Master***[2] as a dressage and jumping horse. I am what is called a Schoolmaster. That means I am kind and helpful and teach riders how to ride. This is especially important for riders trying to learn the higher level movements of dressage that are quite difficult. There are many horses in the world who cannot do these hard movements.

After I teach riders how they are supposed to work with me, we go to horse shows together. This is fun for me. I know

2 *Master*: When talking about horses, this is a person who is highly skilled in the art and science of horses.

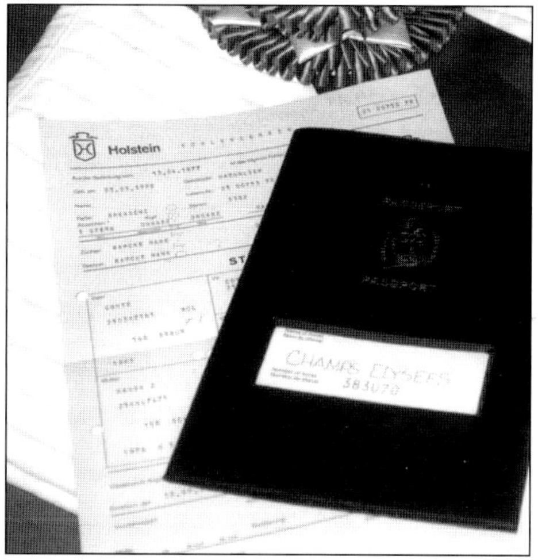

My registration papers and passport.

I am really good and I am quite a show off, but there is something that I love even more. I really love getting turned out in a pasture with other horses and being just "one of the guys".

This way I am free to scratch my buddies' backs and eat grass and think my own thoughts. My owner knows how important it is to let me "have my space", to help keep me from getting tired of horse shows. It is just like when people go to school, they need to have time for learning and time for playing. If we horses get the rest we need, we will be "bright eyed and bushy tailed" for showing!

You will learn about these things and much more as you read through this book. I will teach you a little about how horses feel and think. We will go over the differences between how horses act and feel living in natural vs. ***confined***[3] situations. I want to share with you how horses and people can live together with neither one taking the other for granted. Finally, for those who may buy a horse, I have offered some information on how to begin this process.

Now it is time to turn the page and begin having fun!

---

3 *Confined*: Horses who are in a barn stall, a small fenced in pen, or other enclosed areas and not free to roam around are confined.

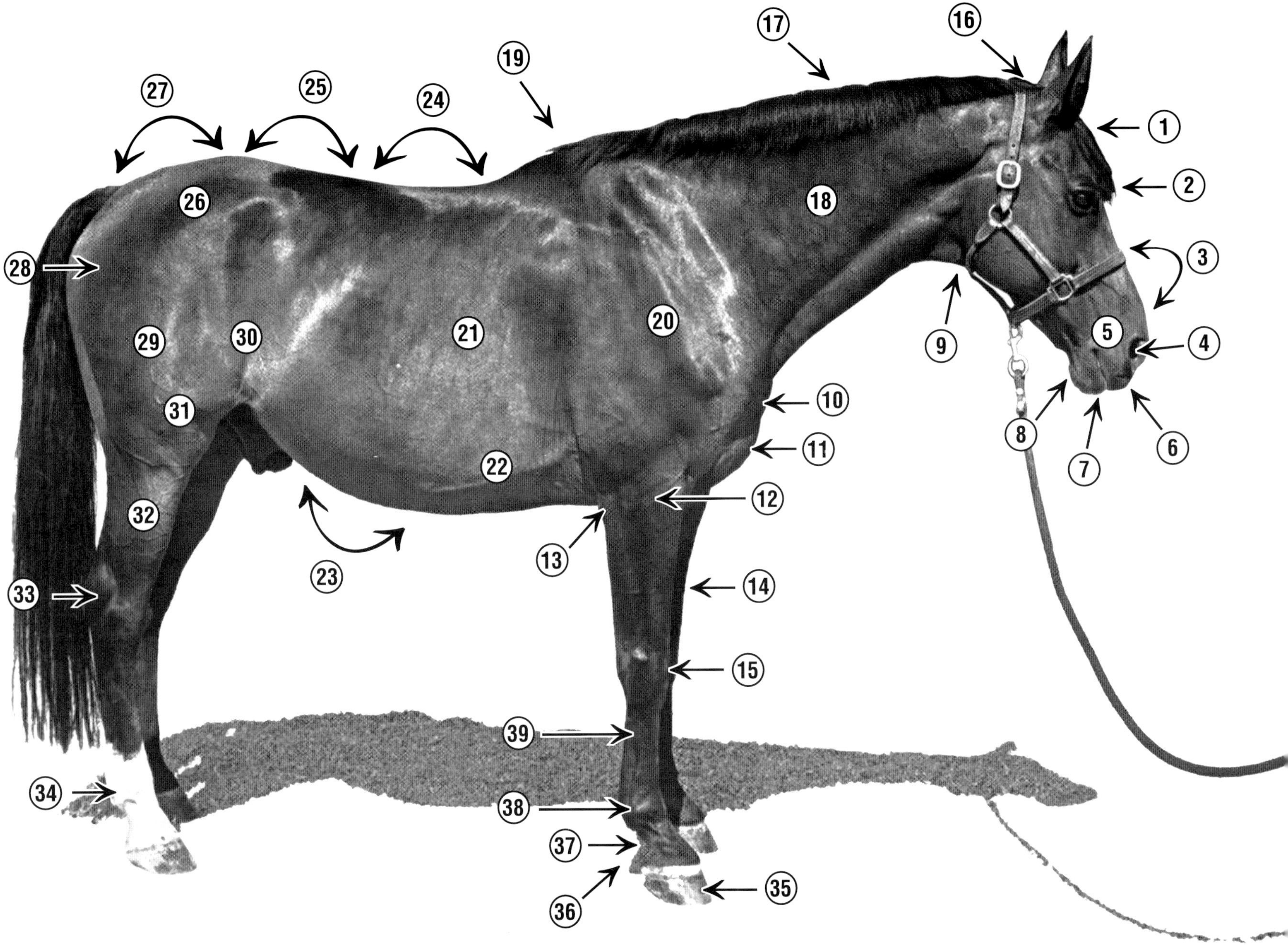
1
2
3
4
5
6
7
8
9
10
11
12
13
14
15
16
17
18
19
20
21
22
23
24
25
26
27
28
29
30
31
32
33
34
35
36
37
38
39

Parts of the Horse

(Shown by Champs)

1) Forehead
2) Face
3) Bridge and Nose
4) Nostril
5) Muzzle
6) Upper Lip
7) Lower Lip
8) Under Lip
9) Throat Latch
10) Point and Shoulder
11) Chest
12) Arm
13) Elbow
14) Forearm
15) Knee
16) Poll
17) Crest
18) Neck
19) Withers
20) Shoulder
21) Barrel
22) Girth
23) Abdomen
24) Back
25) Loin
26) Point of Hip
27) Rump
28) Buttock
29) Thigh
30) Flank
31) Stifle
32) Gaskin
33) Hock
34) Fetlock
35) Hoof
36) Coronet
37) Pastern
38) Ankle
39) Cannon

☑ **Good Job!** *Go to the back of the book and check the completion box for the* ***Saddle Up! Chapter***

Food

My most favorite event is, of course, meal time! I like to sleep and be with my buddies in the pasture. I also like to play, swish tails and scratch backs, but my all-time favorite thing is eating!

In the summer months I spend most of my time on good pasture, which makes me happy since I can eat any time I'm hungry. My ancestors lived on the range and could help themselves when they were hungry, but the "now" generation of horses has been ***domesticated***[4]. Therefore, we have to depend on humans to help us by serving our meals. More and more horses are in confinement situations where they must be fed and don't have the opportunity to feed themselves.

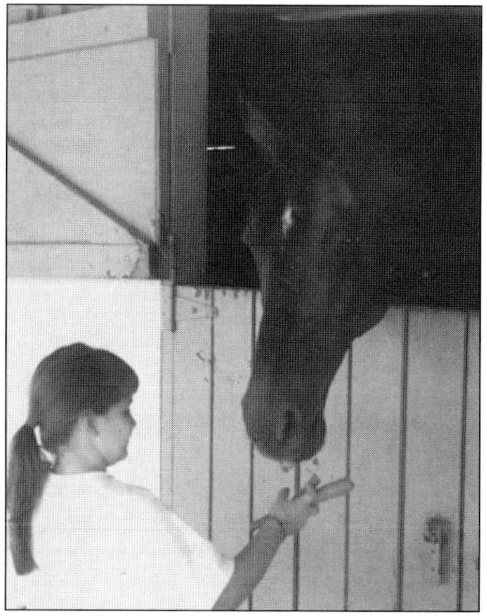

My stomach is small and it can only handle so much food at one time. It was also made to have a steady flow of food going through it. When I am on pasture I eat slowly and

4 **Domesticated**: Tamed from a wild animal.

regularly throughout the day, like horses are supposed to. When humans feed me, good feeding habits are very important, perhaps even more important than my diet.

For example, when I have only one large meal each day, it can create health problems. I should have at least two meals a day, but three or four small meals a day is better.

Let me tell you a little about the different types of food I eat. Then you will understand what I am talking about when I mention them later.

Pasture

Pasture is really an area where I can roam around and eat if there is any food. The food in a pasture is grass as well as other plants that horses like to eat. Other plants we like are trees and bushes with tasty leaves. Sometimes pasture is where humans plant and water grass and other plants. At other times, pasture simply grows naturally from seeds that have fallen to the ground and have been watered by rain.

If you plant your own pasture for a horse, your local U. S. Department of Agriculture office can tell you which would be the healthiest grass to grow for the area where you live.

When your horse or pony spends most of its time on good, healthy pasture, it is getting the daily vitamins and minerals in the form that is most satisfying and enjoyable to it.

Hay

Hay is grass or other food plants that have been cut and delivered to your horse for those times when he or she cannot be on pasture. Hay almost always comes in bales, which means taking a bunch of hay plants and tying them together. These bales can be long and rectangular or round, and will be tied together with wire or string. Hay can also be made into pellets, which I will talk about next.

There are many different types of hay. Most common in the Western United States is alfalfa. There are also many types of grass hay. Hay like alfalfa, which is high in energy, is called rich. Low energy hay, like many types of grass hay, is called poor. Therefore, rich and poor only refers to energy level of ***feed***[5] and does not mean something is good or bad.

How much you feed me depends on what kind of hay you are feeding me. If you feed me grass hay, I need more hay

---

5 ***Feed***: Food that horses eat such as hay, grain, etc.

each day than if you feed me rich alfalfa. A horse or pony who gets the right amount of good alfalfa doesn't need much more than that for his main meal.

This is an important issue to pay attention to, and there is no single correct answer as to how much a horse should be fed. Each horse has its own individual needs, and two horses who are fed and exercised the same will gain or lose weight at different rates. When people talk about a horse who needs only a small amount of food to maintain its body weight, they usually say that horse is an "easy keeper". This means it will maintain its weight or gain weight easily. A horse who must eat more than some other horses to maintain its weight, is called a "hard keeper".

Therefore, if you have the job of feeding and caring for a horse you should pay close attention to how it looks to help you decide how much feed it needs. As a general rule, large animals need more food each day than smaller ones. However, within a group of horses who are all about the same size, some will be "easier keepers" than others.

One thing you should never, ever do is feed me hay with mold growing on it. Eating moldy hay can make a horse sick enough to die. Most horses will not eat moldy hay if a little is given to them by accident. If they are very hungry, or make a mistake and eat some, it can be very bad.

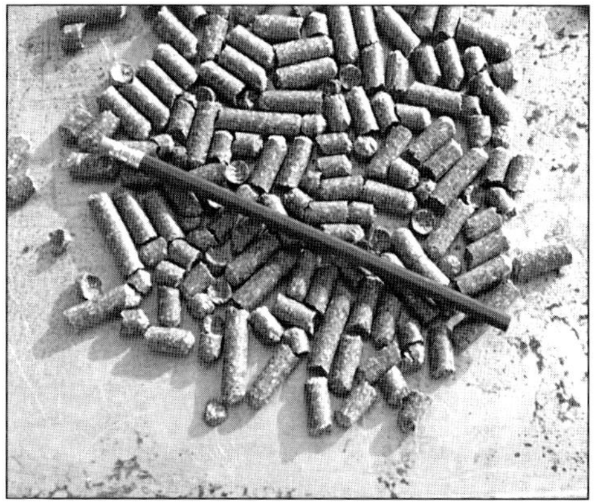

Hay Pellets

Pellets work well for feed in places where there is not enough water or space to grow pastures. You can buy pellets that have grain added to them. Pellets can be fed as a complete meal, or can be fed with hay as well.

I usually waste less when I eat pellets compared to when I eat hay. This is because sometimes I like to eat the most tender parts of hay, and leave the less tasty hay in my manger or on the stall floor.

Because pellets are actually ground up hay, I do not have a choice and must eat them all up. This way I cannot waste as much. One disadvantage to pellets is that they could possibly choke me if I eat them too fast.

Another disadvantage to pellets is they do not satisfy my natural need to chew. Since pellets can be eaten quickly, once I finish them I do not have anything else to chew on. Therefore, I might decide to chew on stalls, fences, or anything else that is nearby.

Grain

Grain comes from plants such as oats, barley, corn, and others which are grown on farms. Grain is rich since it is very high in energy and I personally love it, but it can also cause me problems. If I get the right amount of good hay or grass from my pasture, I really don't need it. The exceptions would be a horse who is a hard keeper, **mares**[6] who are going to have a baby, mares that are nursing a baby, and young **foals**[7]. Also, horses who are working hard, sick horses and horses living in cold winter conditions may need grain for an increased energy level.

Ponies, especially the heavy little guys like Shetland ponies, hardly ever need grain! Adding grain to a pony's diet might only make it fat. If he or she already has a rich diet, adding grain could cause him to **founder**[8]. If you want to give him a treat, a handful of grain won't hurt. He thinks it is candy. But probably an apple or carrot is just as good.

---

6 *Mares*: Female horses

7 *Foals*: A foal is a young horse which can either be a **colt** (boy horse) or **filly** (girl horse).

8 *Founder*: Inflammation of the laminae (a part of the hoof) which is usually caused by over-eating, concussion, toxins released into a horse's body systems from severe sicknesses such as colic, diarrhea, pneumonia, etc.

When feeding grain, ask your **veterinarian**[9] what he or she thinks is good for your horse's or pony's diet.

Also, remember that when feeding grain, add it slowly to your horse's diet. Do not feed large amounts of grain all at one time, such as once per day. Divide the grain and feed it several times per day in smaller amounts.

Treats

Feeding me treats by hand can be good or bad, depending upon the reason you do it. Used at the right time, they can be a great training aid. For instance, if a horse is hard to catch, he will soon learn to come to you if you remember to bring a carrot or a little grain. You will never catch me doing this, but if some horses are given a treat for no reason, it can cause bad manners. They learn to expect a treat from humans and become grumpy if they don't get one. They may even bite or nip at you if they do not get their treat.

---

9 *Veterinarian*: An animal doctor.

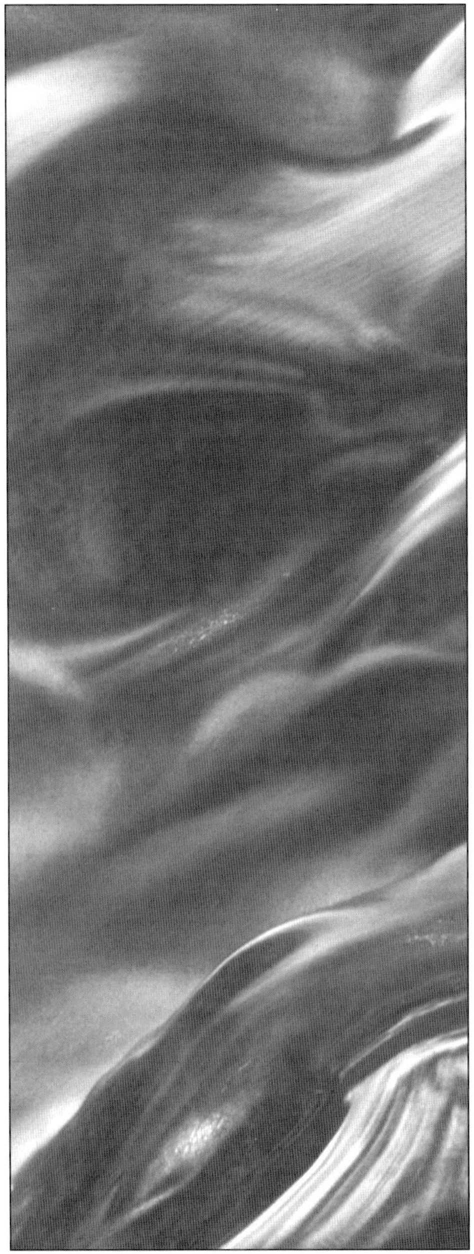

Water & Salt

I should have water available at all times. Horses should always have two to five gallons within easy reach, and depending upon the weather, a 1,000 pound horse may drink from five to twenty gallons of water in a day. I could get by if I got water only once a day, but you can imagine that I would be really thirsty. If I drink when I am too thirsty there is a danger that I will drink too much and get sick. Therefore, it is best for me to be able to drink whenever I wish.

Horses that are sweaty and hot from exercise should not be allowed to drink all they can hold. They should be walked until they have cooled off. During this cooling off time they may have a sip of water, but no more, every few minutes.

I also need salt in my diet. Wild horses will travel many miles to lick salt where there are natural deposits. When I sweat a lot, such as when I am in training and working hard or in the hot summer months, I may have salt leave my body in the sweat. If you make salt available for me, I will eat it as I need it, to replace what I have lost. I always need more salt in the summer than in the winter, or when I am not active.

Salt blocks can be purchased at your local feed store and

will almost always have the proper minerals needed for horses in your area.

This block is made of salt and important minerals for me. You can see that it is different from the salt you may use.

Feeding Supplies

I have a long neck so I can reach the ground when I eat. That is why I like my **feeder**[10] to be low. If it is too low though I may accidentally put my foot into it. To keep this from happening, I could have an overhead feeder, which keeps food up high. While I would never do this, some horses might try to **paw**[11] at these kinds of feeders. If they do, and if their foot gets caught, they could be hurt.

Buckets for feeding and watering should be kept clean. If you use a bucket on the floor for feeding grain, remember to take it away as soon as the horse finishes eating. If you don't, he might put his foot into it and be hurt.

---

10 *Feeder*: What horses eat their food from. It may also be called a manger, feed bin, or hay net.

11 *Paw*: Hit with a front foot.

How The Food Moves
Through My Digestive System

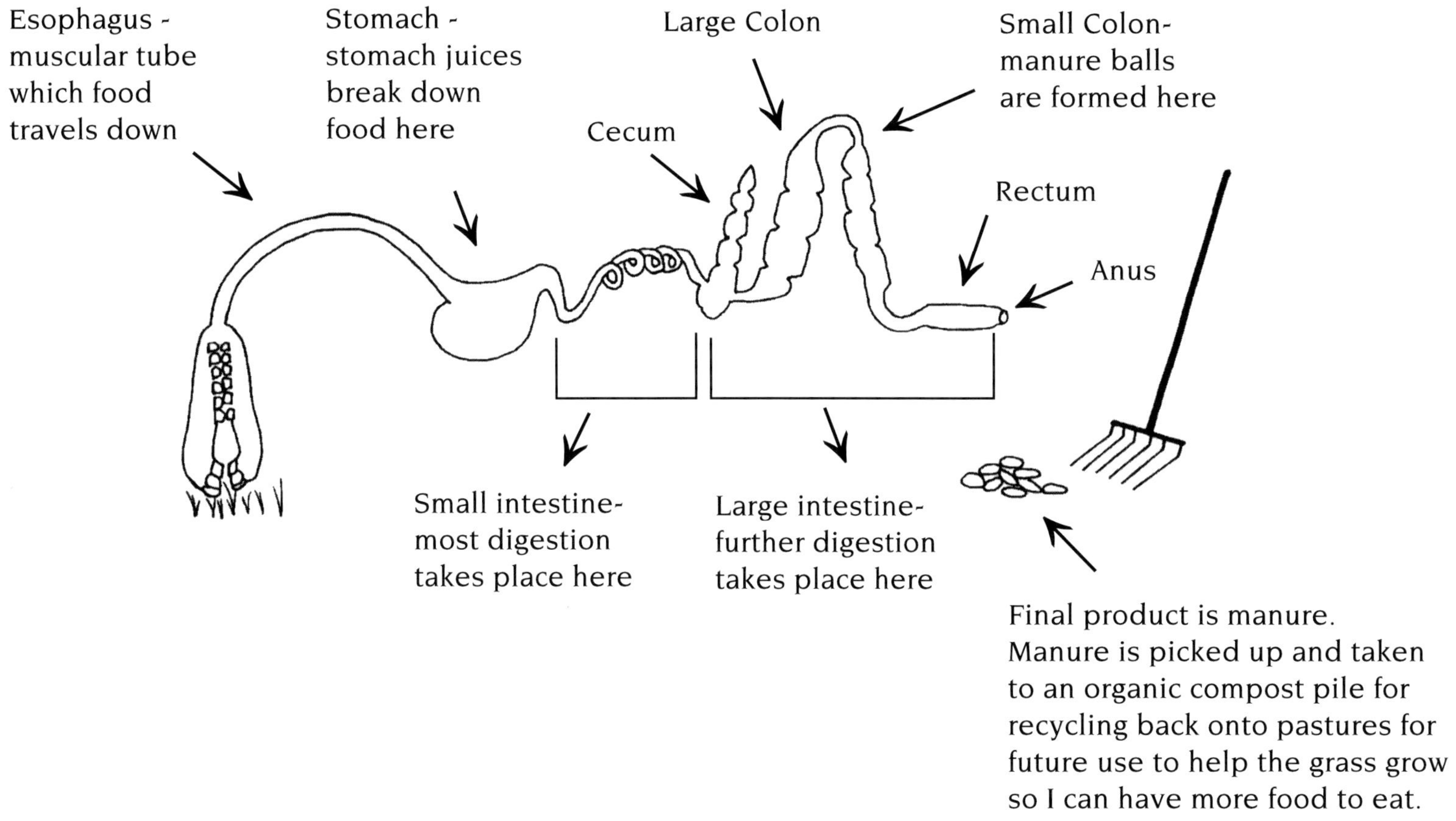

Good Job! *Go to the back of the book and check the completion box for the* ***Food Chapter***

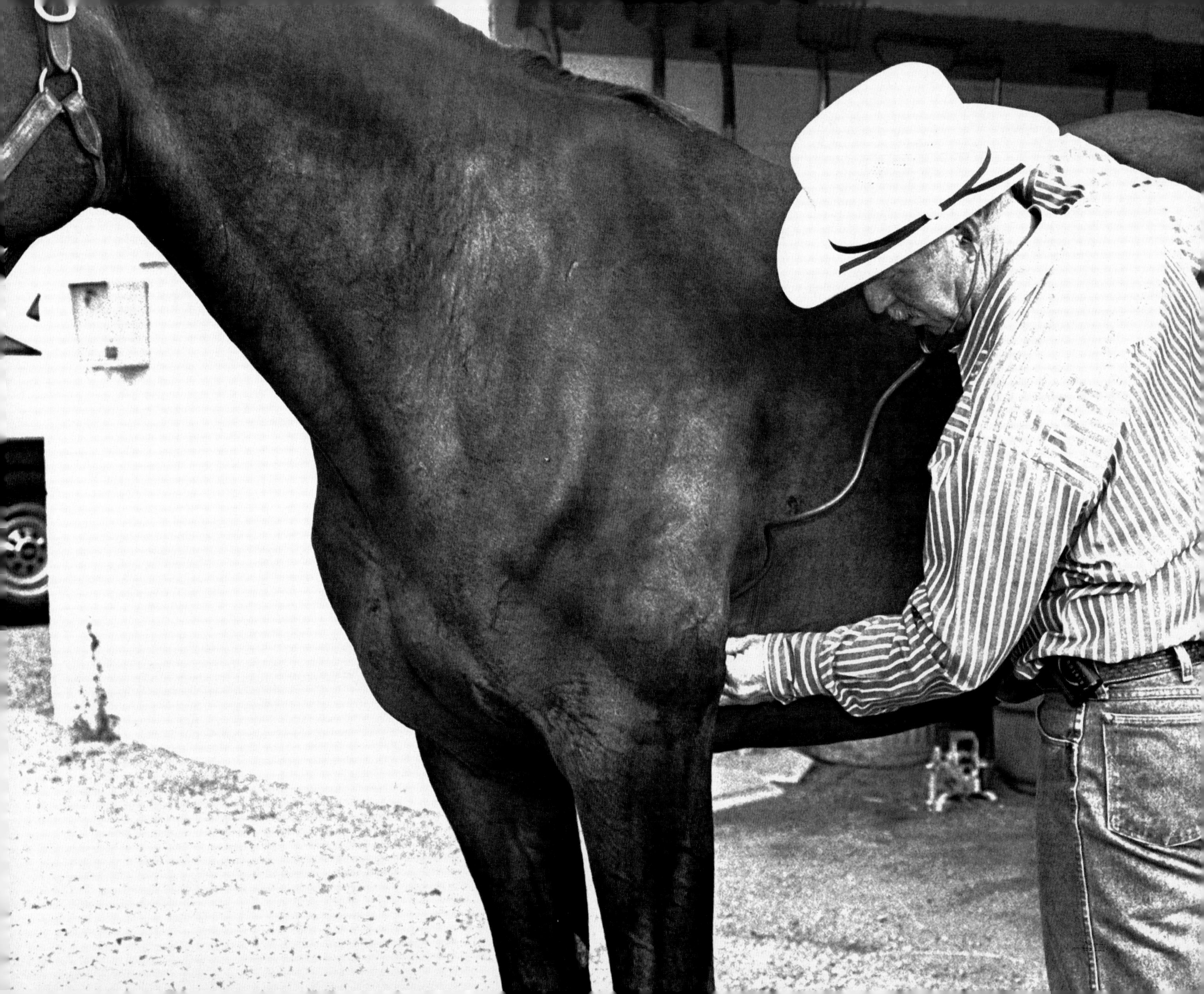

Health

A very important human in any horse's life is a good doctor. I need to have regular check-ups just like you, and if I get sick or hurt I need someone to help me get well again. This person is called a veterinarian.

Veterinarians are also called vets. I think that is because "vet" is easier to say. I know it is easier for me to say.

Some vets only work with large animals like me, and others only work on small animals like dogs and cats. Because of this, it is important to me that when I need a doctor I get a vet who knows as much as possible about horses. Believe me, that is not always easy.

Usually you can find a vet by asking someone who owns a horse. If you do this, you should know the person well and trust what they say. You can also ask someone at a nearby riding stable or at a professional training barn.

Let me tell you a little about what my vet does for me. My

Humans play a big role in keeping horses healthy.

Vet trucks usually have almost everything in them needed to help animals. They become a traveling Doctor's Office.

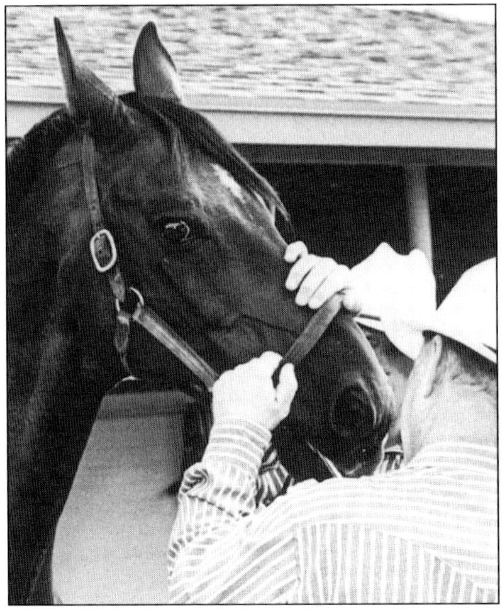

vet helps decide what foods I should eat to keep me healthy, helps find a good **farrier**[12] to keep my feet and legs working properly, and checks me all over two times each year. Another thing the vet helps watch for is worms.

It may seem strange, but horses can actually have worms which live inside them. When this happens it is the vet who helps get the worms out.

When I am really sick, my vet may give me drugs to help me get better. This will only happen when I cannot get better by myself and I need some help. Just as with humans, drugs can help when I need them, but they can hurt if they are not used the right way.

Maybe you are beginning to see how important vets are. That is why you should find a good vet before you buy a horse. This may sound funny, but if a horse has any health problems, you will want to know what they are before you buy it. This means that you want to have a vet you trust give the horse a health check-up before you ever spend your money. Also, make sure the vet you use is not chosen for you by the person who is selling the horse. That would be called a conflict of interest!

12 *Farrier*: A person who puts shoes on horses and cares for their feet.

Healthy is as Healthy Feels

I love to be healthy and feel good. Keeping that way is the same for me as it is for you. Good health depends on the food I eat, getting the right exercise, having a safe place to live, and not catching a sickness from another horse. In other words, prevention is the best medicine.

This also means that humans play a big role in keeping horses healthy. It is up to humans to pick out healthy food and feed us regularly. They make sure we do not eat too much at a time and do not go too long between feedings. I must have exercise, but it should always be safe. You probably know all this already. At least you would if you thought about it a little. This is called **common sense**[13].

These things all help keep me from getting sick. Sometimes I get sick anyway and you need to know it. I cannot tell you I am sick, but there are ways you can tell if

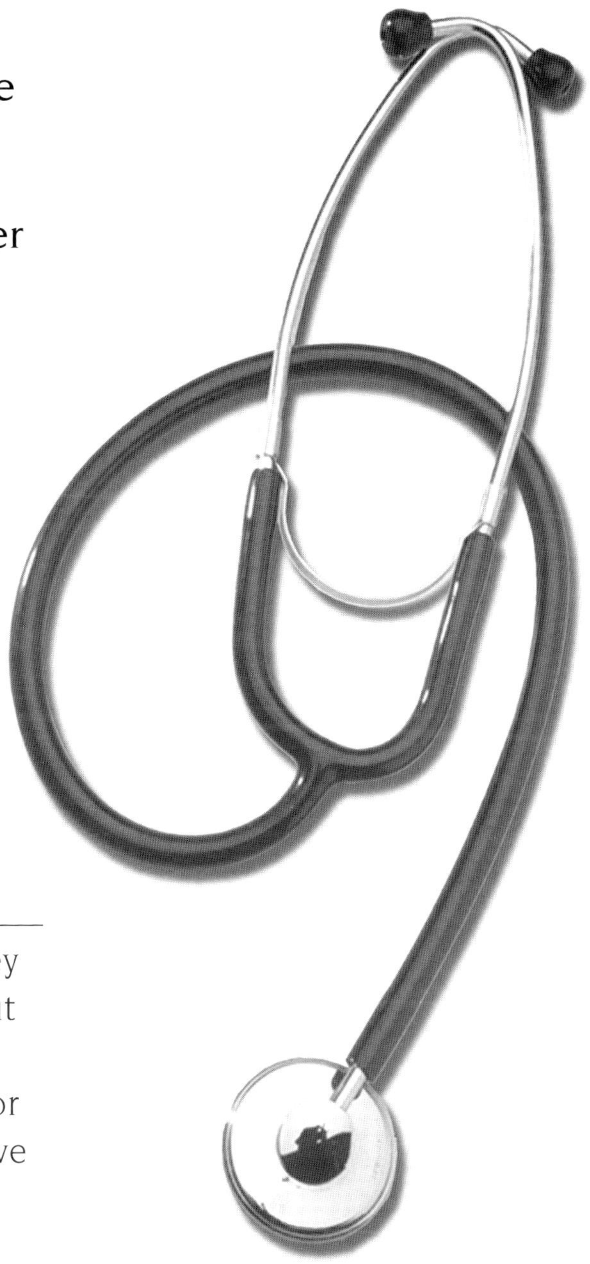

13 *Common sense*: When a person thinks about something which they have little or no knowledge of, and comes to a logical answer about how it works, how to act, how it will respond, etc. this is called "common sense". For example, if you think about it, it is smarter for you to exercise in a safe way than in an unsafe way. You do not have to know all about exercise to make that logical conclusion. This is common sense.

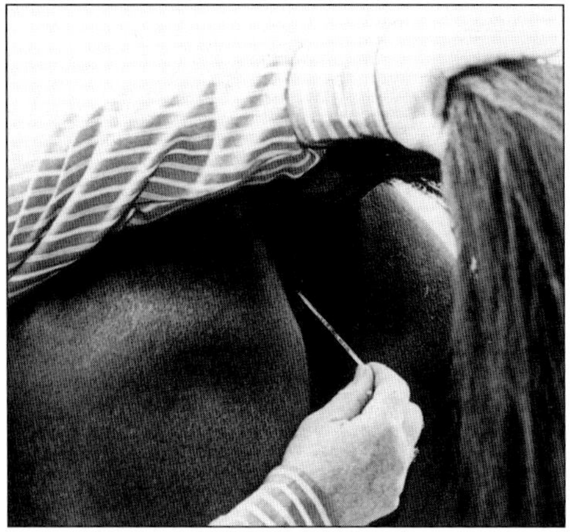

Taking my temperature with a thermometer can help you know if I have an infection or virus.

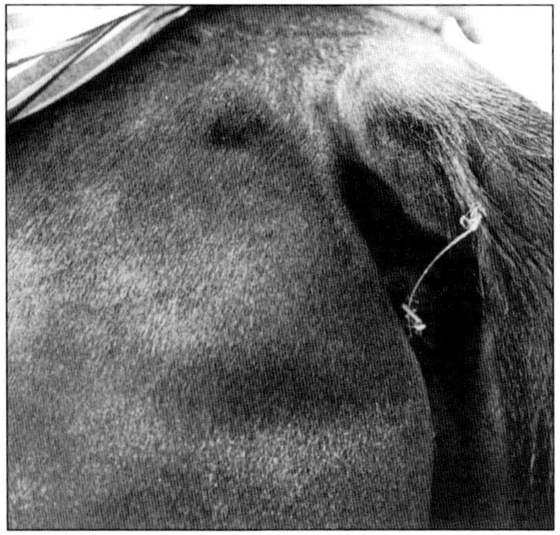

Once the thermometer is put in, it is secured to the tail with a clip until the temperature has been taken, then it is removed.

you try. For example, taking my temperature with a thermometer can help you know if I have an infection or virus.

My owner knows me very well. She knows how I act when I feel well. If I start acting differently, she knows something is wrong. Just as when your parents know when you are feeling good or bad, she knows when I am.

So how can you tell if a horse feels bad? Look at how they act. If you treat me well I will say hello to you by nickering when I see you. If I do not do this, I might be sick. I might also hang my head down low if I am sick.

Check to see if I am eating well. If I leave food in my manger or refuse to eat, I am upset at something or I am sick. Think about how I act when you are around me. If I am usually active and wide awake, then one day I look sleepy, I might be sick.

I can have a runny nose and not be sick. I do not cry like you do. My tears come out my eyes *and* my nose. That's right, I actually have tear ducts in my nose! So if you see a runny nose that is clear, it is probably because my eye is watering. But if I have a runny nose that is yellow or green, I am sick. White discharge is usually a sign of allergies.

Horses can also get bad stomach aches called colic. When horses have colic they may bite at their side, or look at their side, or kick at their tummy. They may also swish their tail in a circle, or lie down and kick their feet. If you see a horse do any of these things, it may need your help.

Colic usually happens because food stops moving through my tummy. This can happen from eating too much or not drinking enough water when I eat dry hay. It can also come from eating and drinking when overheated, like right after exercising. Or, it can be because of worms in the stomach.

When I get sick I cannot throw up and get the bad things out of my stomach. Because of this, I could die from a stomach-ache. This means that if I have colic, it is an emergency and I need a vet quickly.

The best thing a horse can do while waiting for the vet is to stand or lie quietly. However, the pain from colic is very, very bad. When horses try to stop this pain you will see them kick, roll on their back, or lie down and kick at their stomach.

The best thing you can do is give them is a painkiller.

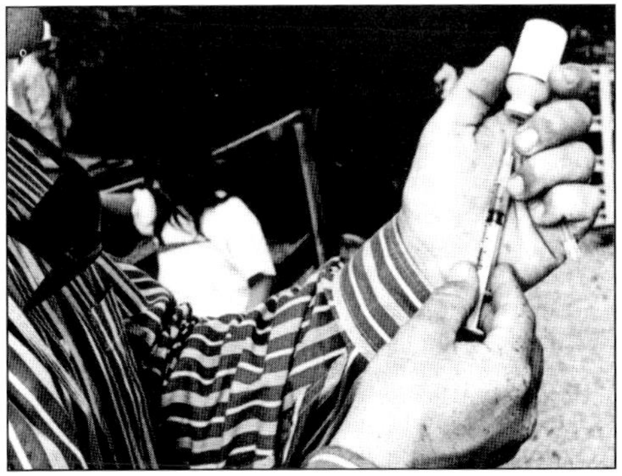

My veterinarian makes sure I have all of my shots. Here, he is getting ready to give me a shot.

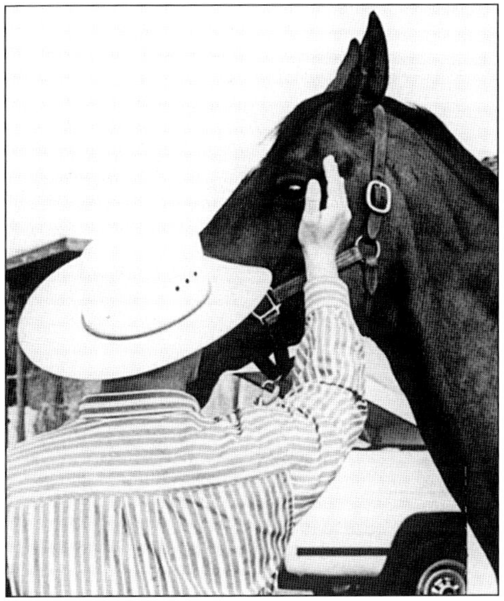

Notice that the Veterinarian Assistant holds his hand behind my eye. This can keep me from seeing the needle going in, because I can be frightened of shots, just like you.

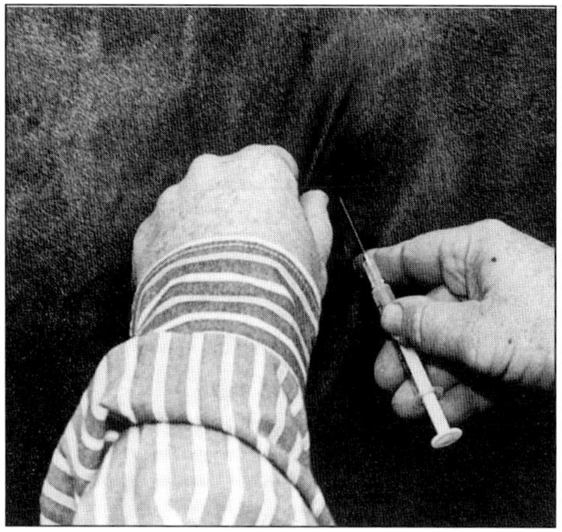

This works for you when you have a headache and your parent gives you something for it. If you cannot give them a painkiller, you should lead them slowly and keep them walking. The exercise will give them something to think about instead of the pain until the vet gets there.

If I stand in an odd way it could mean my feet or other parts of my body hurt. Normally I stand with one hind foot tipped to rest one of my hind legs. I also rest one hind foot then the other. If I do not switch feet this way, something is probably hurting me in my foot or the leg that I am resting.

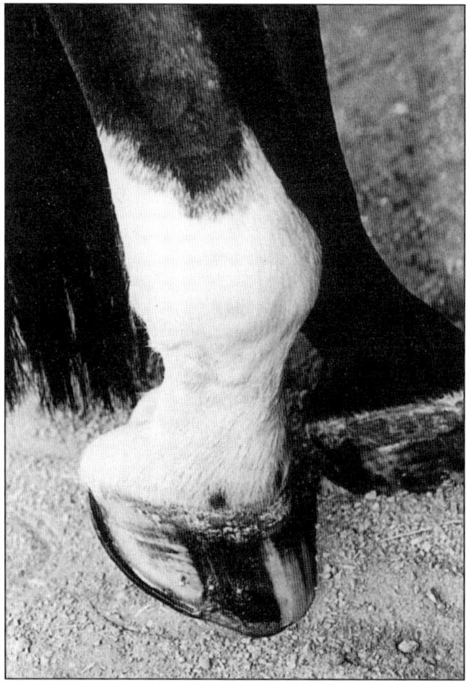

If I stand in an odd way it could mean my feet or other part of my body hurt.

If I act this way you should check my foot for **thrush**[14], or maybe there is a nail in the bottom of the foot. Another possible problem might be an **inflammation**[15] of the laminae of the feet. This is usually caused by eating too much. This problem is called founder, or laminitis.

Inflammation can also give me problems in other parts of my body. Any time I have swelling or heat somewhere on my body, it could mean I have inflammation.

---

14 *Thrush*: An infection in the bottom of the foot.

15 *Inflammation*: This can mean many things. When a part of the body becomes swollen and hot, infected from bacteria, or painful, it is called inflamed.

A dull, rough coat is another sign of poor health. If my hair is not smooth and shiny, pay close attention to any other possible warning signs we have talked about.

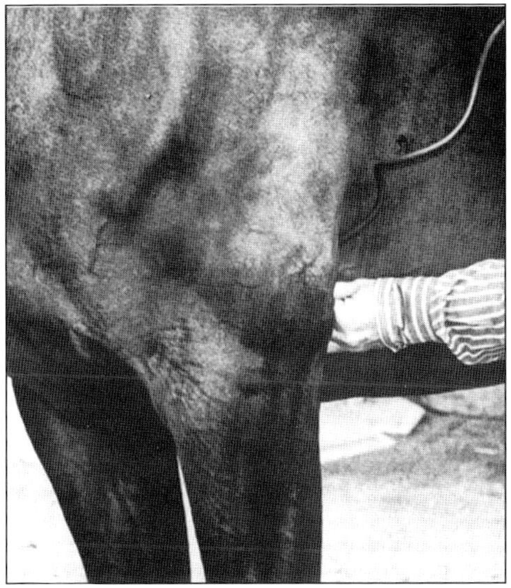

If I am breathing fast, like a dog panting, it could be a sign of pneumonia or heaves. These are both sicknesses of the lungs and need a vet's attention quickly.

Another way you can tell if a horse is not feeling well is by looking at his or her manure (when you were young you probably called this poop). I know, yuuuuccchh. However, this can tell you a lot about what is going on inside a horse's stomach. In fact, many parents do this with their children when they are babies to make sure their stomach is working well.

Horse manure should come out like firm wet balls. If a horse has dry hard manure, it could be that he is not getting enough water to drink. Very runny manure or diarrhea could be signs of a sudden change in his feed or a stomach problem.

Another way my human keeps me from getting sick is by getting me a check-up by my vet. In these check-ups, the vet will check my teeth, my feet, my legs and my ears. I get my temperature taken, and everything else looked at that a human can think of.

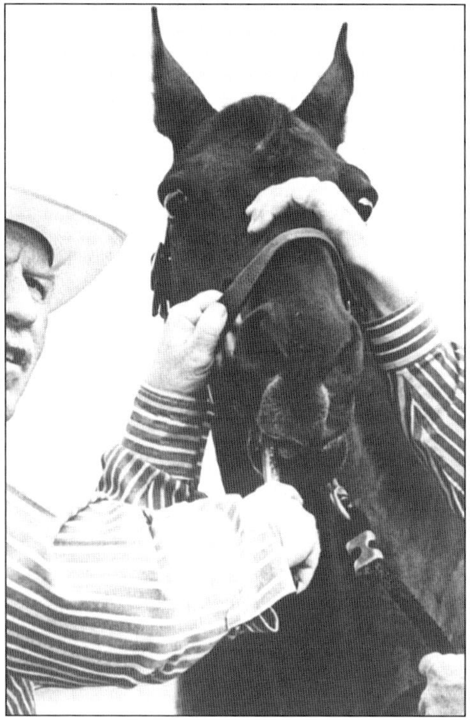

My teeth form sharp points on them which can hurt my mouth and make it painful to chew. My Vet smooths my teeth with a large file to fix this.

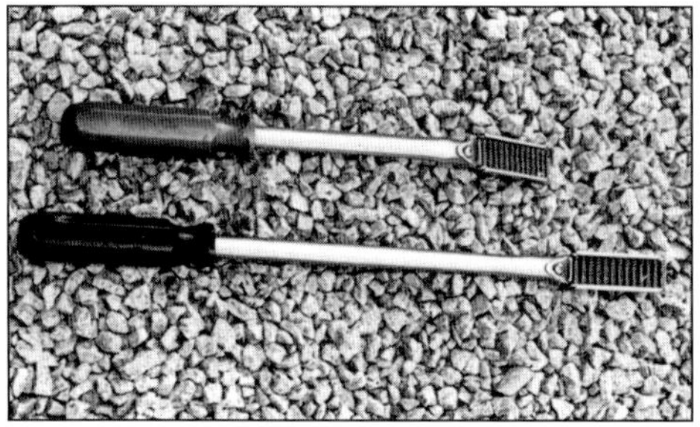

My veterinarian also makes sure I have all of my shots. These shots include tetanus, just like humans get, and other shots for sleeping sickness and influenza (the flu). Some horses need shots for certain sicknesses that are in their area. If this is true for your area, your vet can tell you what they are.

Remember when we talked about worms before? These can be a major problem. There are several types of worms I may get, and my vet will either give me medicine to get rid of these harmful worms or will leave medicine with my human to give me every once in a while. For most horses, once they get worms, they never get rid of them for good.

Some of the pests humans call 'worms' are not even worms at all. Sometimes worms are actually fly **larvae**[16] which look kind of like worms but are really not. Either way, everything humans refer to as worms can be harmful since they all live in my body somewhere and actually eat parts of me. That's right, they will either eat my blood or parts of my insides, and they may either move out of me through manure or may

16 *Larvae*: When flies are in their youngest stage of life, many of them live in the form of a worm-like creature called a larvae. These larvae later change into flies. A similar process takes place when a caterpillar turns into a butterfly.

live a long time inside me.

Horses usually get worms by eating the worm, its eggs, or a larvae. These can be on grass in their pasture, or in stalls or stables where horses live. Once a pasture or stall gets worms living in it, about the only way to get rid of them is to keep all horses and other animals away for a long time. This keeps the worms from getting into a new horse. Then the worms in the pasture or stall die.

Wild horses had less of a problem with worms because they were always moving from one place to another. This way they could always eat fresh grass which did not have any worms on it.

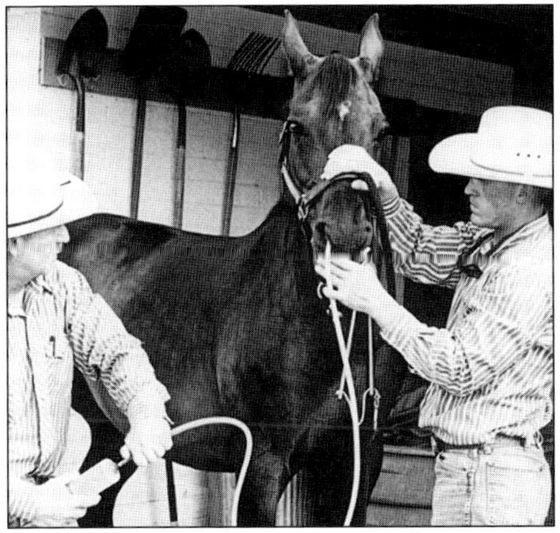

There are several types of worms I may get. Here my vet is putting medicine directly into my stomach with the help of a tube. Notice that the tube goes through my nose. From there, it goes down my throat and into my stomach. (My vet really likes his job, you can tell from the smile on his face!)

☑ ***Good Job!*** *Go to the back of the book and check the completion box for the* ***Health Chapter***

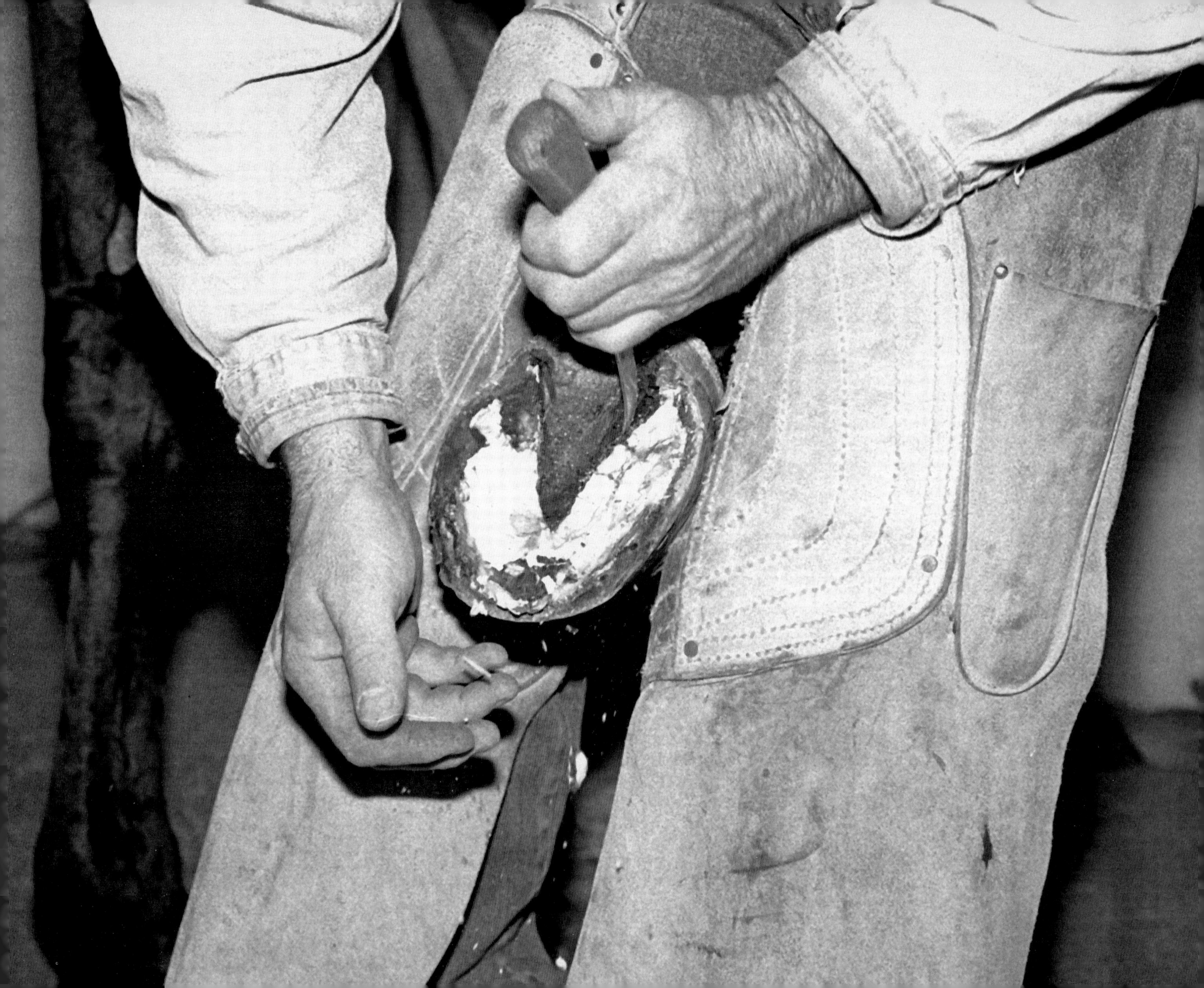

Shoeing

My feet are called hooves. They are one of the most important parts of my body and actually can help pump blood. I will talk more about that soon, but let's discuss other things first.

My feet are important because I must be able to walk. You can imagine that I cannot do this very well if my feet do not work. Since I am so heavy, I put a lot of pressure on them, and even though they are designed to take this stress, they need to be taken care of well.

The outside of my hoof is very much like your fingernail, except it is much thicker. Also, just as your fingernail has no feeling, neither does this outer shell. On the other hand, inside my hoof I have many fragile bones just like you. My bones are not shaped the same as yours, but they can hurt just like your foot can hurt if someone steps on it. These bones are held in place by ligaments and tendons. They are cushioned and padded by cartilage. I also have a foot part called the sole, which is also hard like a fingernail and is the

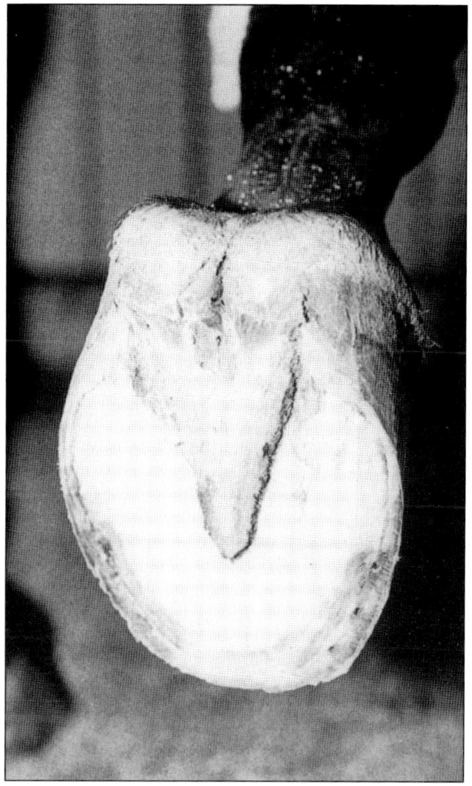

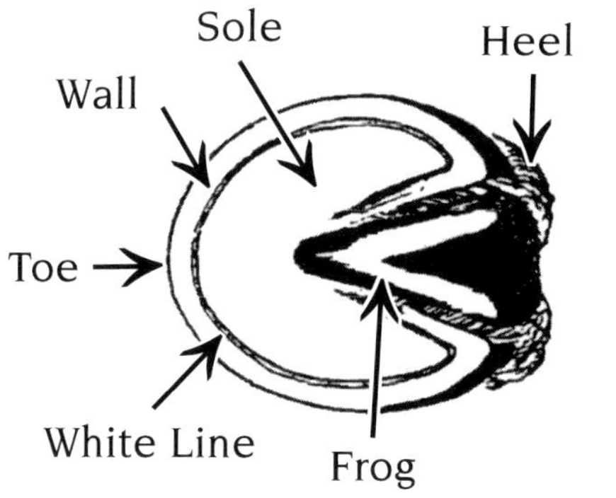

The parts of the bottom of my hoof.

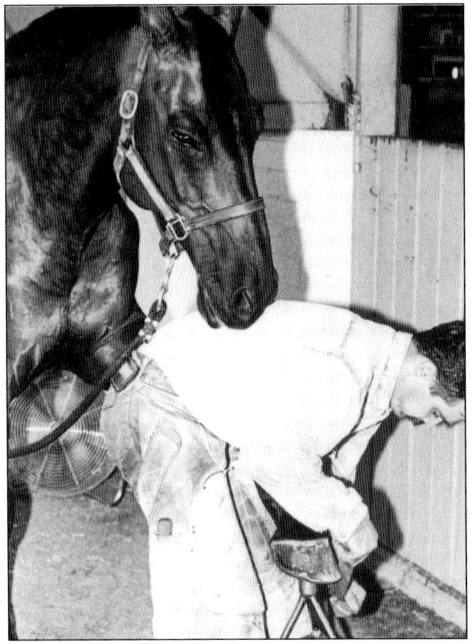

bottom of my hoof.

A truly amazing part of my foot is a small area on the bottom of the hoof called the FROG. That's right, it is called a frog! Can you imagine that? It doesn't look like a real frog unless you use your imagination, but this area is very important. In fact, it is so important it is often called the "second heart". This is because it is kind of soft and allows my foot to flex, or move a little, each time I step on the ground. When my foot moves in and out like this, it actually pumps blood through the small blood vessels in my hoof the same way my heart pumps blood. Therefore, it is called the second heart.

Remember when I said the outer hoof part was like your fingernail? Well, it grows just like your fingernail too, and must be kept short enough to let my frog touch the ground when I step. This is what helps keep my feet healthy.

Long ago when horses roamed freely, their hooves were kept short naturally because the ground they walked on wore them down. When horses can't do this because they are shut into a stall or for any other reason, their hooves must be trimmed by a farrier. For most horses, this needs to be done about every six weeks. If my feet get too long my frog could shrivel up because contact with the ground is no longer possible.

Not only does this cause poor blood circulation, it also can cause problems in my legs, shoulders and hips. This is because these body parts must absorb the shock my feet should be taking, and they are not designed to do that. Any problem that keeps me from walking or traveling well is called unsoundness.

We trust that you will keep our feet in good shape. A good way to do this is by using a farrier who will maintain the natural form of our feet, realizing that each horse's hoof is individually different, just like human feet are.

You can see, then, that farriers are very important people in our lives. A farrier is actually someone who puts shoes on our feet, but this is no simple task. They must know all about what makes a hoof healthy or unhealthy. Since they can actually change the angle of our hoof in relation to our legs, they must know how these changes can help or hurt us.

Some farriers will actually make our shoes out of steel. When they do this, they will form the shoe properly to fit our foot, make holes through the steel shoe and actually nail it to our foot with special nails called horseshoe nails. Other

Here are some of my Farrier's tools.

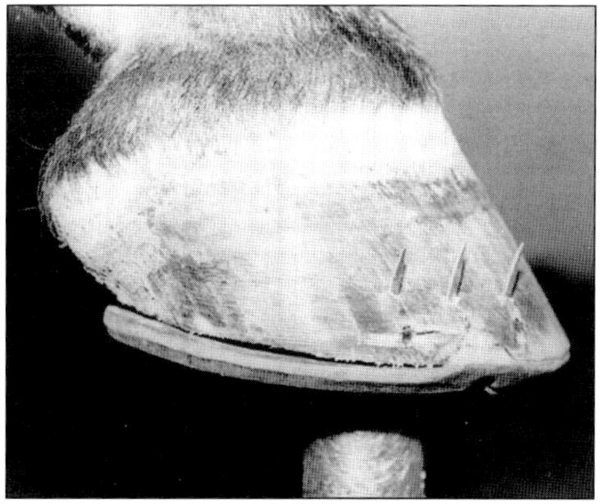

See the nails in my hoof. Next, the farrier will cut them off and bend them over to keep the shoe on tight.

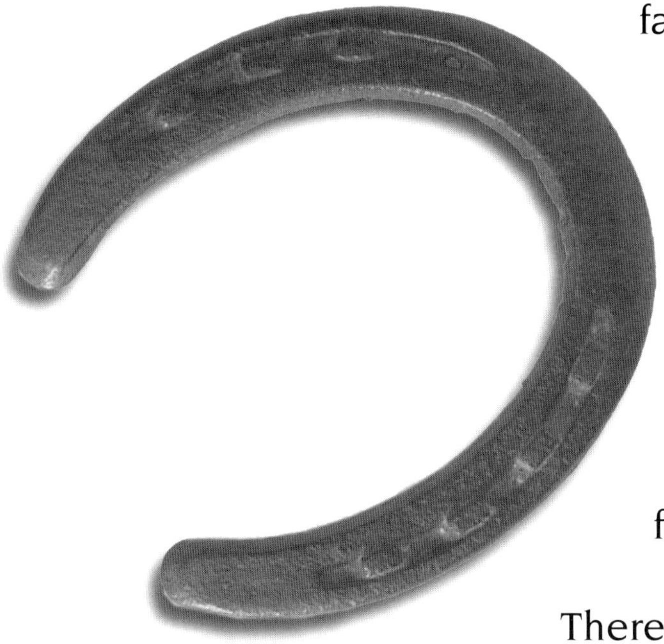

farriers may buy shoes that have already been made, complete with nail holes. These shoes only need to be shaped and they can be nailed on.

This can sound strange to people who have never heard of it before, but remember that there is no feeling in the outer shell of our hoof and nails are actually the best way to keep our steel shoes on our feet. However, if a farrier makes a mistake and lets one of the nails go into the wrong place in our foot, it can hurt, bleed, and get infected.

Therefore, it is important to have skilled farriers work on our feet. It is your responsibility to make sure they have these skills. Your veterinarian can help a great deal in choosing the right farrier for your horse.

Some Fragile Parts Inside My Foot and Leg

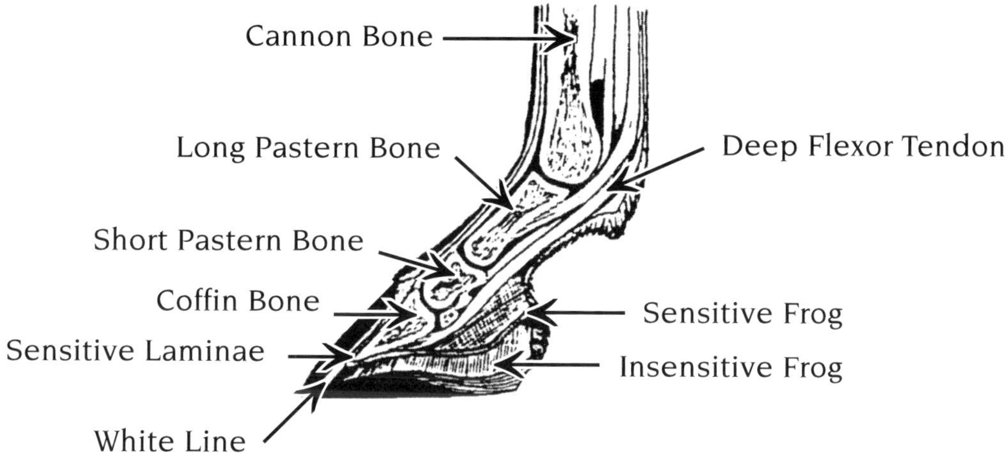

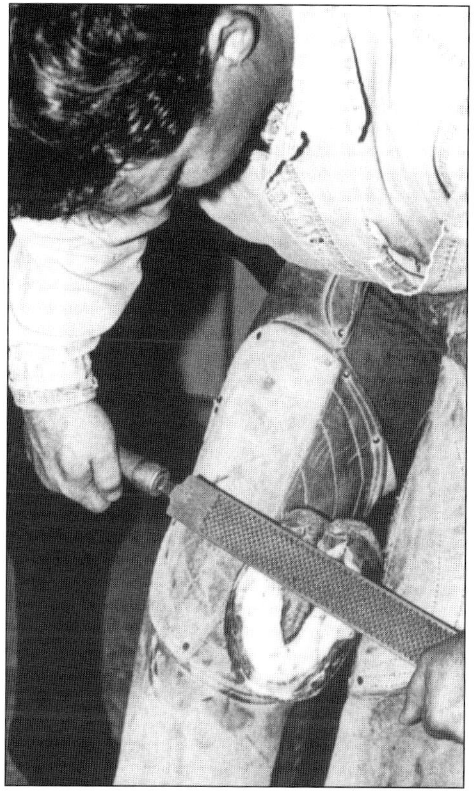

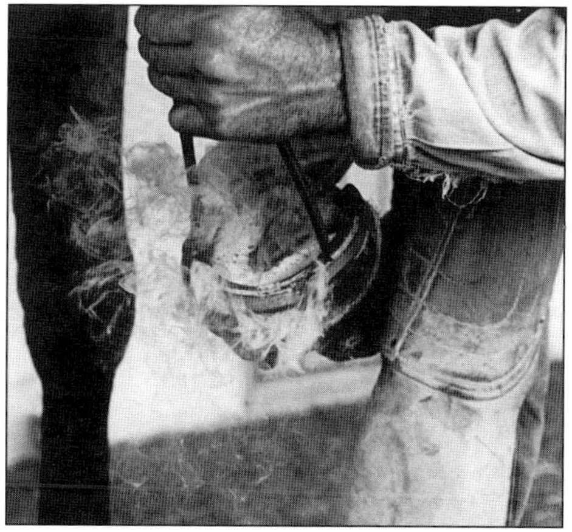

☑ **Good Job!** *Go to the back of the book and check the completion box for the* ***Shoeing Chapter***

Grooming

Grooming? What is grooming? Your parents might say it means brushing your hair and taking a bath. They are right. It is also a very important part of feeling good and being healthy.

For example, horses are like many other animals that grow long hair in the colder part of the year in order to keep warm. When the warm temperatures come again, we need to get rid of all that hair to keep from being too hot. The way we do that is by grooming, and this helps us feel good.

If I am shut in my barn, my human has to help me get this hair off by brushing me. If I am out on pasture I get this hair off by rolling on the ground. Can you believe that? I can roll in the dirt and it is good for me! Not only does it help get my long hair off, it also relaxes my muscles, scratches any itches, and chases any bugs off my back.

My friends and I will also help groom each other. You can see me in the pasture with my buddies having a scratch

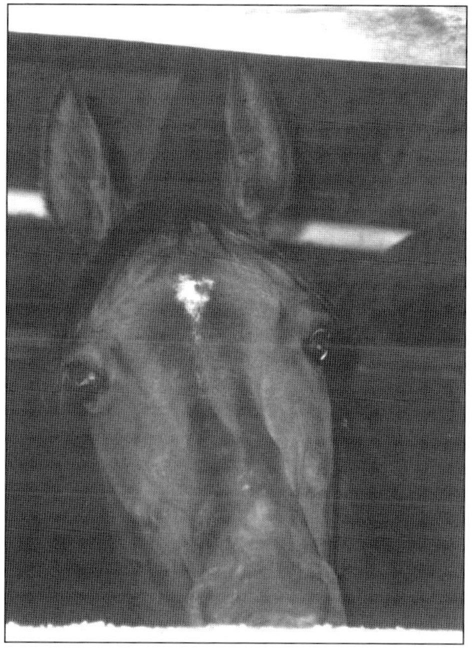

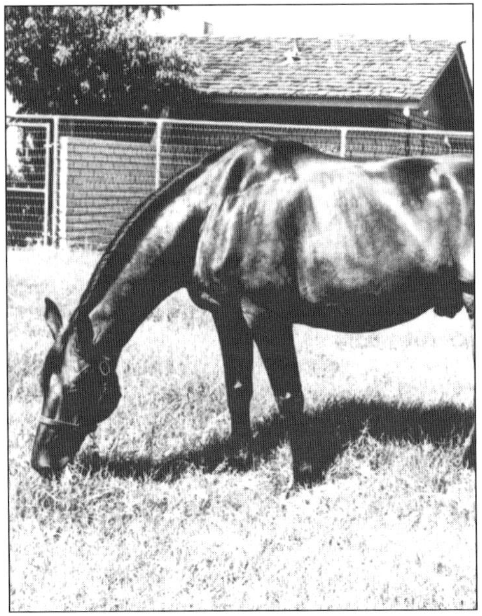

session with our upper lips stretched out scratching each other's backs. This is one of my most favorite times, almost as good as eating!

If I am out in pasture most of the time in the winter, I only need to have the surface dirt taken off in grooming. If you clean me too well, you might take away protective oils that help keep me warm and dry.

When I am working and being ridden regularly, all the rules change. Then I need all the dirt off me. If I have dirt on me when I get ridden, the saddle might rub the dirt against my skin and make sores. I also look better when I am working at a horse show if I am clean and shiny. This only comes from good grooming.

My human **body-clips**[17] me in the winter and keeps me in a warm, toasty barn. When my hair is short like this it is very easy to keep clean, but horses that are clipped must be blanketed each night if it is cold, or we can get sick. The only reason to body-clip a horse is if they are going to be shown. It is better if horses can keep their own hair and maintain their body temperature naturally.

---

17 *Body-Clip*: This is when the hair all over my body is cut short.

In the summer time my coat is short and very fine, and more time is required for grooming me. After my owner rides me, she washes off the sweat and dirt that I get from the exercise. Heat builds up under the **saddle**[18] and **bridle**[19] and can cause sores on me if I am not cleaned in the areas that the equipment has come in contact with. She has to be careful, though, if she washes me off on cold or windy days, I could get sick.

Good grooming makes me look better, just like it does you! My human takes pride in how I look and makes me feel and look good. But, sometimes, she's not so smart. She gives me a bath and then she turns me out and I go quickly to the mud hole and lie down. Boy, it's the greatest feeling in the world being covered with mud!

---

18 *Saddle*: What a rider sits on when riding on a horse's back.
19 *Bridle*: A bridle is used by the rider to control the horse. Bridles are made of two parts, a headstall and reins. The headstall is made of leather straps which goes around a horse's head from behind the ears to the mouth. At the mouth, it connects to a metal piece called a bit which fits inside the horse's mouth. The reins are long straps which go from the bit to the rider's hands.

CURRY COMB

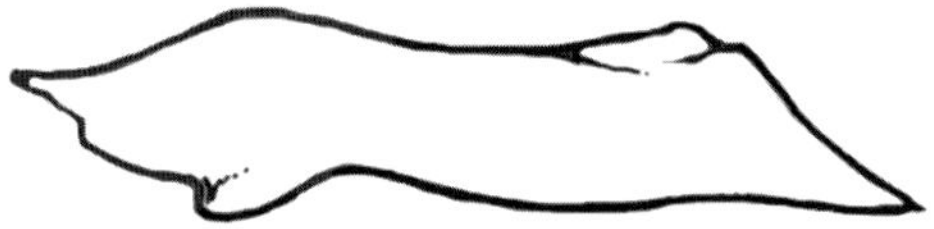

GROOMING CLOTH

DANDY BRUSH

Tools

Good grooming tools also help improve my circulation and tone my muscles. One tool is called a curry comb. These come in many shapes and sizes and are used to loosen dirt. They should be used gently in a circular motion against the direction in which the hair grows, loosening the dirt as you circle around and around. Where the mane grows out of my neck, my withers, and along my back to the beginning of my tail is where I love to be curried. Curry combs are not used below the knees and hocks, or on the face where bones are thinly covered by the skin because they can hurt.

These areas should be cleaned with different tools. The face, eyes, ears, nostrils and lips should be gently washed with a clean sponge or cloth. A dandy brush is used to clean the lower legs.

Dandy brushes are course and rough, and some horses do not like them. If a horse has sensitive skin, dandy brushes may scratch them too much. For other horses, you can use dandy brushes on their whole body. Dandy brushes help penetrate the hair for a deep clean after the curry comb is used to get the top layer of dirt off.

The body brush is used after the dandy brush to add a

special polish to the hair or coat. You can use the body brush instead of the dandy if your horse has tender skin.

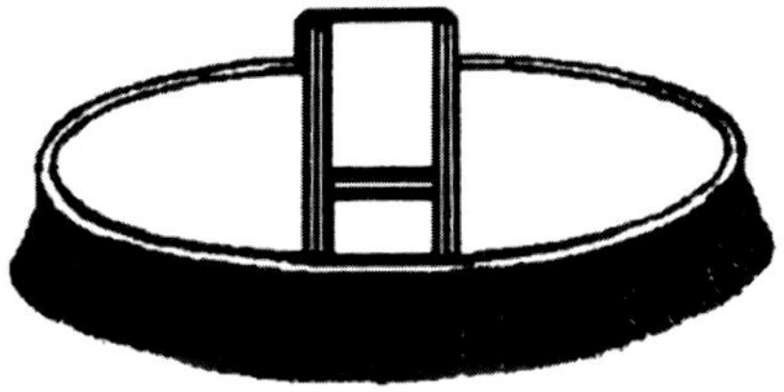

BODY BRUSH

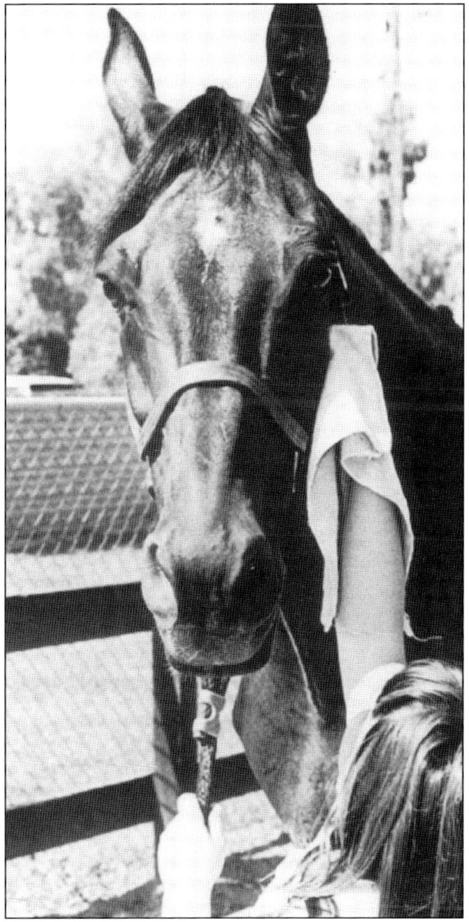

People should also be careful when brushing horses on the parts of their body where they do not have much padding. For example, my backbone and face bones do not have thick padding from muscle and skin. If someone presses too hard on these parts of my body, it could scrape and hurt me, just like if someone were to brush you hard along your backbone.

Horses are very ticklish around the belly and back legs because the skin is very thin and tender there. Horses get upset and can even kick at the groomer if they get too rough in grooming this area.

Another tool is a sweat scraper. This is used to remove water after you have washed off your horse. This helps me dry soon after my bath. Then there is the rub rag, or towel. This is used to remove the last bit of dirt and to put the final shine on my hair.

My mane and tail are long hair that can stay long summer or winter. The mane comb is used just like you would use a hair comb to get the tangles out of your hair.

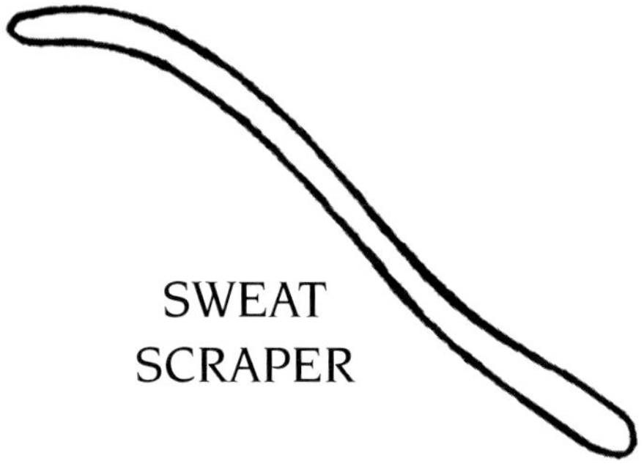

SWEAT
SCRAPER

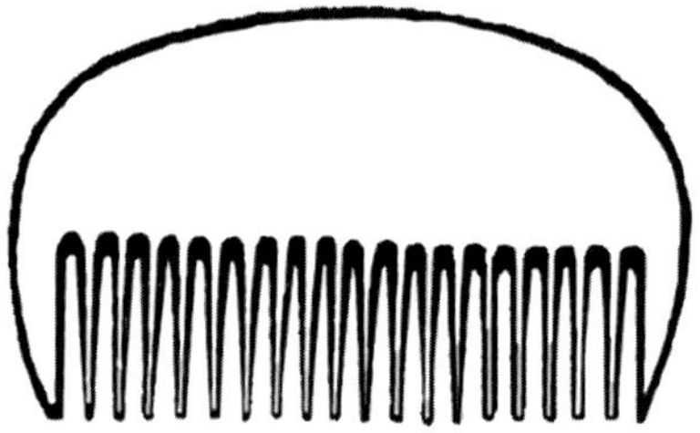

MANE & TAIL COMB

My owner uses a mane comb to pull my hair and keep it short. This makes it easy to braid and look pretty for shows. Other types of show horses might need to have their manes kept long, and never need to be pulled. When my ancestors ran the range, their manes were only pulled short by tree limbs and brush. Mostly, their manes were long and fell on both sides of their neck. This helped protect the neck from the weather and bugs. Once humans got into the act, they began to train the hair to fall only on one side of the horse. I suppose it looks neater this way and doesn't get in the way of buckling the **throat latch**[20] of the bridle.

A hoof pick is used to keep dirt and manure from getting between the frog and the sides of the hoof. When I have horseshoes on they hold more dirt and manure in the foot than if I did not have them. After riding, my human uses the hoof pick to quickly check my feet to make sure I have not picked up a rock or stick from exercising. In fact, any time a horse starts limping, always check its feet. It may have stepped on something and have it stuck in the foot.

Another reason to pick my feet daily is to keep me from

20 *Throat latch*: A part of the bridle which goes under a horse's neck, from one side of the head to the other.

getting something called thrush. This is a disease I get if my feet are not kept clean and dry. You know your horse has thrush when the bottom of the foot has a very stinky odor and you can scrape black, wet 'goo' from between the frog and the side of the foot. If not taken care of, thrush can cause a horse to go lame. Then it will need the care of a veterinarian.

HOOF PICK

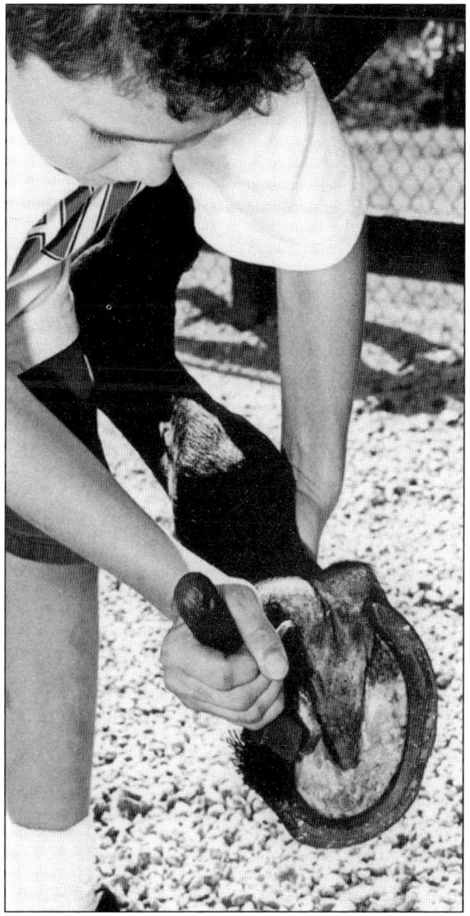

Good Job!** Go to the back of the book and check the completion box for the **Grooming Chapter

Sleep and Rest

Sleep and rest are as important to me as they are to you. Just like you, sleep helps me conserve my energy and is good for my emotional health. Have you ever been grumpy and tired in the morning because you did not get enough sleep the night before? I am the same way, except I do not need as much sleep as you. For example, humans sleep about 8 to 9 hours per day, but horses need only 3 to 5 hours per day.

When horses are out on the range, like wild horses or horses from a cattle ranch, they are always walking about in search of food. In the summer months when there is grass everywhere, they can sleep more because they are not so busy looking for food. When winter comes, there is not as much grass. Then these horses have to walk around more, looking for food, and cannot sleep as much.

Since there are animals like mountain lions, who hunt horses for food, this is another thing that determines how much sleep wild horses get. To make sure these animals do

Lying down lets our bodies totally relax. Horses need this just like humans.

not eat them, wild horses will sleep for a very short time, then wake up and eat a little, then sleep a little more.

Because we know we may have to wake up quickly and run from these types of animals, horses have learned how to sleep standing up and lying down. That's right, we can do it either way! When we sleep standing up, we have muscles and something called a stay apparatus in our legs that lets our legs lock into position so we can sleep. This is not like any lock you have ever seen, but it works for us just the same.

We do not really rest very well from this "standing up" sleep, but it does rest us a little bit and is called the "sleep of the mind". In order to rest really well, we must lie down and sleep, and we try to do this for at least a little bit each day. When we lie down and sleep, it is referred to as the "sleep of the body", and is more of a deep sleep.

Horses need to lie down to allow their bodies to totally relax just like humans do. If I do not get to lie down when I would like, I will be very tired and can become cranky just like when humans don't get their proper sleep. My human knows how important this is so she makes sure that I have enough space in my stall to lie down.

This is especially true at a horse show. Traveling to horse shows can upset me, and working very hard once I get there can make me very tired. This means I need to rest every chance I get. Any time my human and I go to shows, she always makes sure that my stall is big and bedded well enough with shavings or straw to let me lie down when I would like.

Another interesting thing about horses like me who live in a stall is that we sleep more than horses who are on pasture or in the wild. In fact, we often sleep during the night, just like humans. I think this is because our humans usually do not ride us at night so we know we won't be bothered by them.

I can sleep standing up by simply locking my legs into position.

Well, I really don't use a key, but I bet you can get the idea anyway!

Good Job! *Go to the back of the book and check the completion box for the* **Sleep and Rest Chapter**

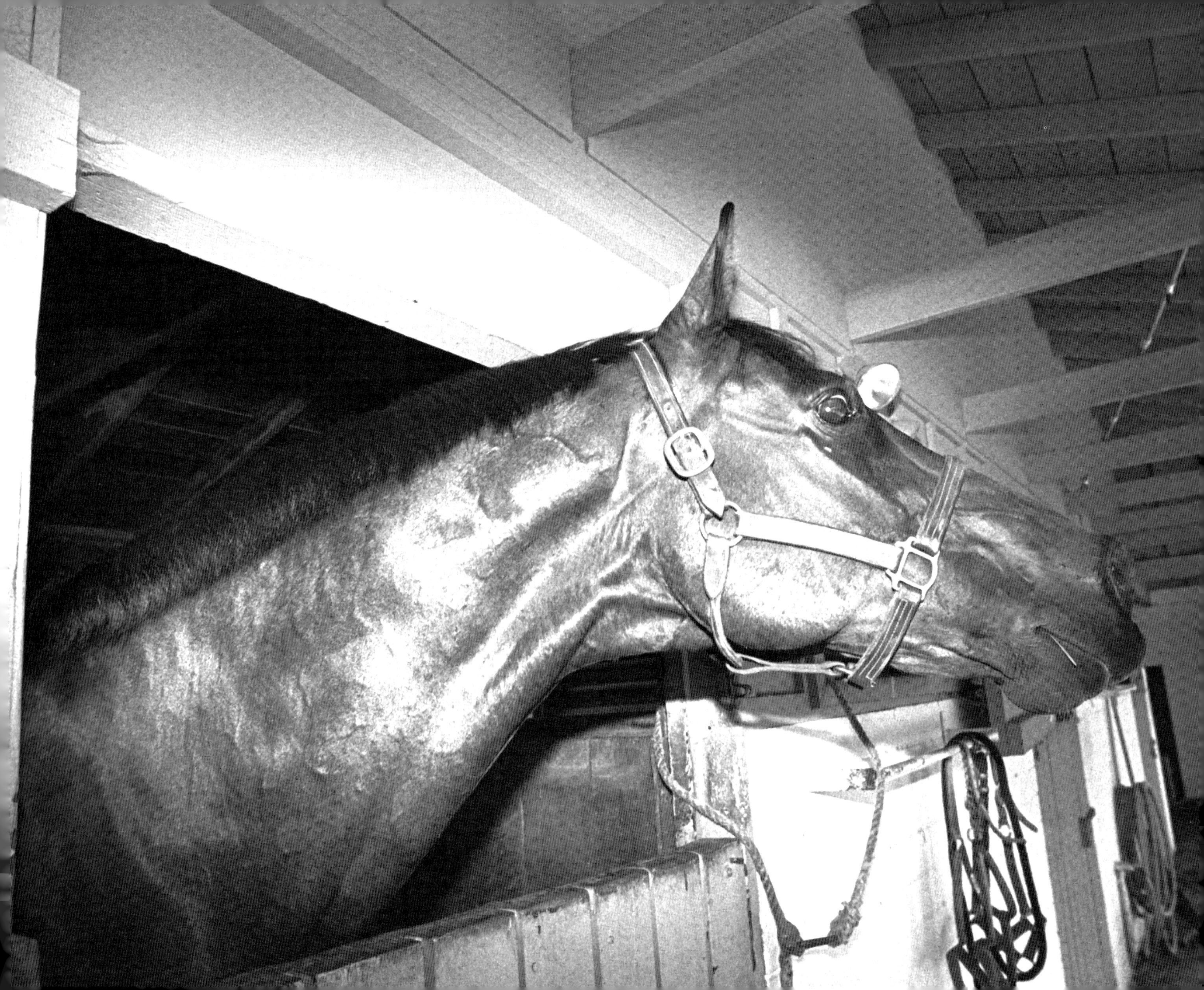

Behavior

Behavior means how someone acts. If you know how horses will act, it helps you be safe when you are around us. That is why I think this is the most important chapter. Please read carefully and learn all you can. Also, if there is something here you do not understand, please ask an adult to help you. I *am really serious about this.*

The first thing to learn is that all horses are different, just like people. Just because one person acts a certain way does not mean another person will act the same way. The same is true for horses.

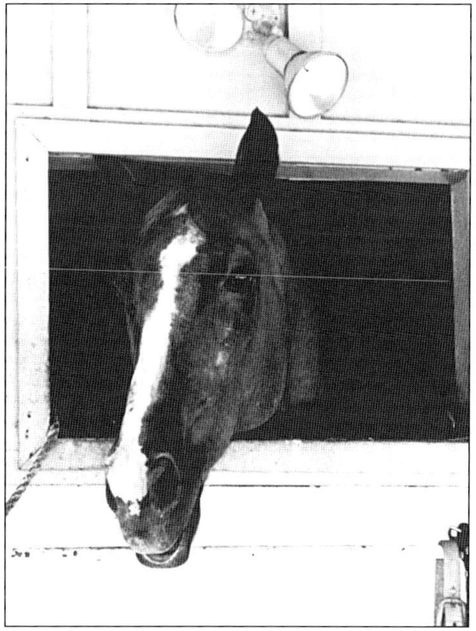

There are some things that are the same of all horses, but first, let's talk about horses being different. Some horses are very calm, almost like they were born that way. Other horses seem like they were born always afraid. It is possible that you know of many differences like this between people. All these differences apply to horses.

Now think about what would happen if a horse who is

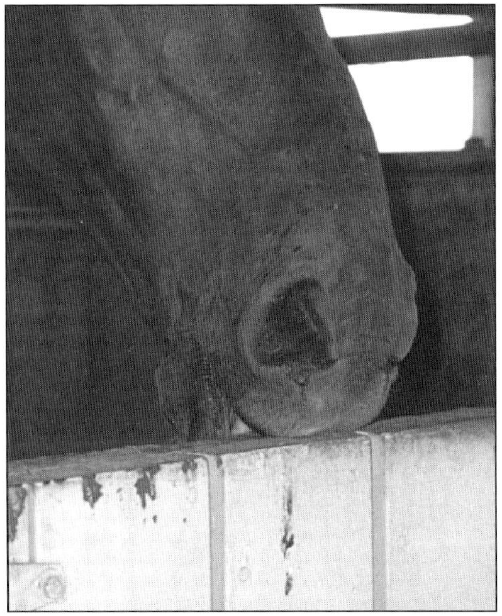

always afraid is treated in a mean way by a person. I think that horse may try to run away any time a person comes near. If they cannot run away, they might try to hurt the person to keep from being hurt themselves. You should *always* be very careful around horses. We can be the best friend ever, but it is smart just to be safe.

Some horses will also act differently from one time you see them to the next. This can be because something in the horse's life has changed.

For example, there are some basic things I need to keep me happy. If I seem to be unhappy, it could be because these needs are not being met. If I am unhappy, I may begin to act strange and do things that you might think are bad manners. These bad manners are called **vices**[21] by people.

We have already learned about how I am usually happy being outside eating grass. When I am locked up in a stall, some of my important needs are not met. I can become

---

21 *Vice*: A wickedness, or other behavior which people are frightened by or do not understand. This can also refer to a "bad habit" or action which a person simply does not like. An example of a bad habit which is harmless to humans, is when horses chew on the wooden parts of their stall.

stressed, or worried, and this is when vices can begin to show.

When humans see a horse chewing on the stall door, or sticking their tongue out and making faces, they may think this is bad behavior. They need to understand that the horse is only reacting to the stress and trying to live within unnatural surroundings.

You can see similar things in humans who have stress in their lives. They might chew their fingernails, eat too much, or do something else that is not always good for them. While people will allow this for themselves, they think it is not good for us to do the same. This is because sometimes horses can hurt people by their vices such as biting, or kicking. Then humans punish us for this behavior, which only makes us more stressed.

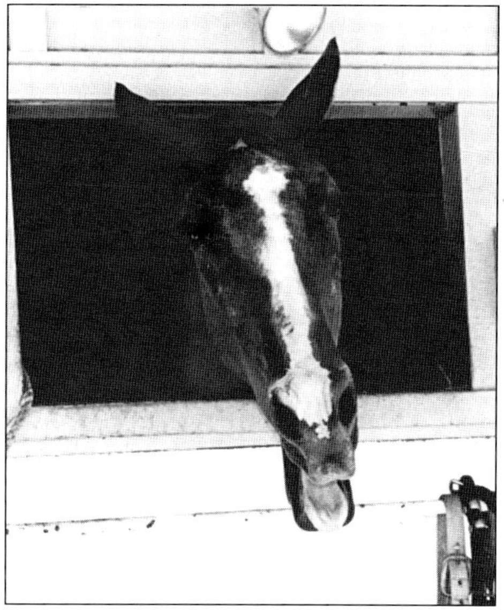

The best thing for humans to do would be to think about why we act the way we do and try to make us more comfortable. Horses, just like humans, want to be physically comfortable. For most horses, comfort comes from eating, drinking and having shelter. We like to rest and sleep when we want. Also, we want to move around and explore our surroundings. We are territorial, which means we like to have an area we can call our home, and we like to be free

to move around in it.

We are a social animal, which means we need to have friends. Scratching another horse's back and having our back scratched by another horse is an important part of friendship for us, and we need friends. We also like to stand side by side and 'head to tail', and brush flies from each other's faces with our tails.

We also like to just travel around and graze (eat grass). Wild horses may travel up to 6 miles per day and spend 2 to 3 hours in travel time as they graze. As we travel, we can bond with other horses. Humans do this when they get together and talk to each other just to be friends.

We also form a herd order or a pecking order. This is how we know who the boss of the herd is. Once we have done this, the boss will decide where we go and when we go there.

One of the reasons people love us so much is because we are able to run fast, and they get a sense of freedom when they ride us. This speed lets us get away from danger when we see it. Some people even say that all horses are creatures of flight, meaning that we usually run away from danger. However, if we cannot run, we can be wicked fighters.

These 'flight or fight' skills are also learned when horses are free to roam. We act our fighting out by playing with our buddies, or we pretend we are wild horses and run.

Another area that plays an important role in our behavior is our senses. Like all other animals we have senses for seeing, smelling, feeling, tasting, and hearing. We use these senses to get information about what is happening around us. We use this information to decide how to behave about things.

Of course we feel good when we are groomed, and this gives us comfort. We will smell to help find out if we should be afraid of something. We also smell as a way to show friendship. If you walk up to me and I smell around your face, I want to be your friend. Smell and taste work together to help us choose the best feed. It also helps decide if we are about to eat something poisonous.

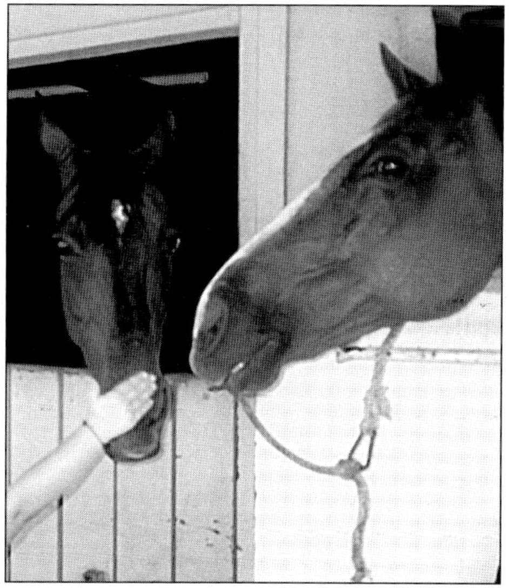

Horses see much differently than you. Our eyes are not made like yours, and the shapes we see can be much different than the shapes you see. Some people think horses are being silly when they are frightened by something they see. They just do not understand that it looks scary to a horse.

Another reason we can be frightened by what we see is

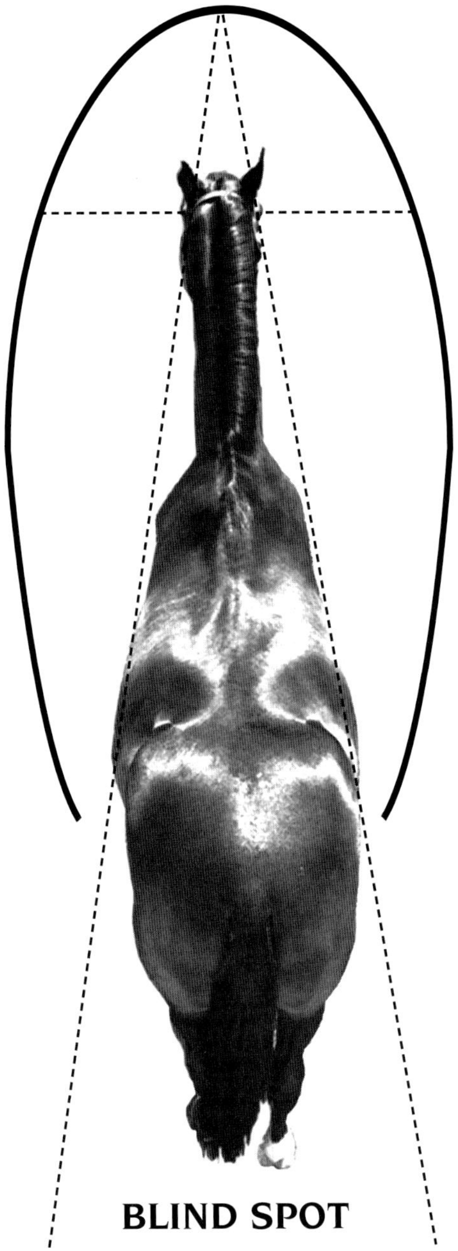

Range of Vision of the Horse

My eyes are spaced widely apart on the sides of my head. In fact, I often look at one thing with my right eye and a different thing with my left eye at the same time. This is called **monocular vision**. *When I look directly forward, I see things with both eyes at the same time. Seeing something with both eyes is called* **binocular vision**. *This picture shows you how this works for me.*

You can tell from the picture that each of my eyes can look at something from right in front of me, all the way along my side to a point almost directly in back of me. Since my hips block my vision directly behind me on each side, there is an area back there in which I cannot see anything unless I turn my head. This is called a blind spot. Also, when I look forward with both eyes, it is hard to see things which are close to the front of my face. I even have a hard time seeing what I am eating.

Think for a moment, what it is like for me when something moves suddenly from the blind behind me, into my vision on one side. Since it is to the side I will only see it with one eye, and could easily be frightened badly. When horses are frightened they sometimes run away quickly or even kick out at whatever causes the fright. These are behaviors you should watch out for.

that our eyes are placed on the sides of our head. This allows us to see one thing out of one eye and a different thing with the other eye at the same time. This is called monocular vision. We also see only a little color. As a result, we can get confused and frightened by what we see and decide either to run away or attack by kicking and biting.

A really cool thing about having eyes on the sides of my head is that I can see almost completely to the rear and on both sides of me at once. While this is helpful for horses out on pasture to see danger all around them, if you walk up and surprise me, I might get scared and kick out at you. *This is why I say that people should always say something to a horse when they walk up to them*. Even if it is just something simple, like 'Hello horse'. If you do this, I can tell who you are and it helps keep me from being afraid.

As you can imagine, my hearing is very good. One thing that helps my hearing is the way my ears are made. I can point them both forward or backward at the same time, or I can point one each way. Pointing my ears like this lets me hear what is happening in front and in back at the same time. It is really hard to sneak up on me.

Horses can also tell you things with their ears. When we decide to fight we will look at whatever is making us angry and put both ears straight back. If you ever walk up to a horse who has both ears back and looks unhappy, you should be very careful, or not go up to them.

So you see, by pointing our ears back this way, we let you know what we are thinking. This is kind of like talking to you. Another way we 'talk' is by neighing, grunting or crying. We neigh to say hello to our friends. We can grunt when we are about to eat and we cry or squeal when we are playing or fighting.

Our emotions can also effect our behavior. We feel pain, hunger, fear, anger and excitement, just like you. We feel

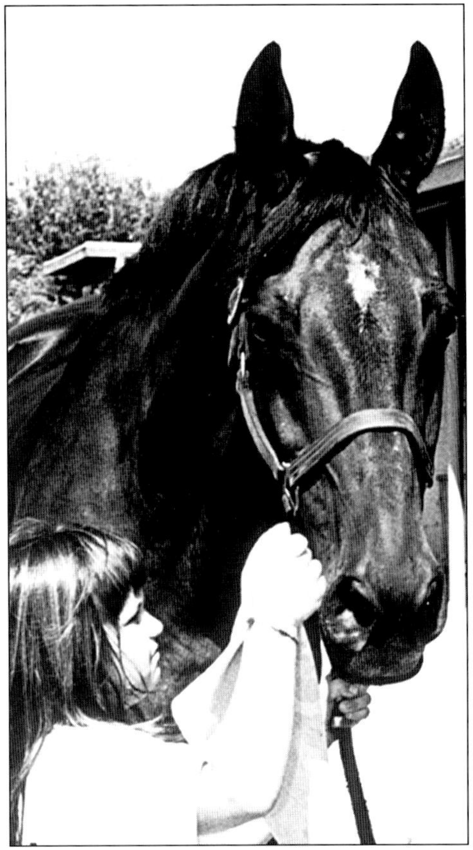

lonely when one of our friends goes away. All of these feelings can cause us to behave differently than you would normally see us.

Horses pay close attention to people when they are near. We can tell when you are nervous or frightened and that can cause us to behave the same way. Some horses even seem to enjoy teasing people. They can do this by watching to see if you are nervous around them and then act in a way to make you more nervous. You can believe me when I say that we can control how you see us and what you think of us.

When a horse is lazy and does not want to work, it will pay close attention to its rider. If the rider does not seem to know how to make the horse work, they will go very slow, not turn when the rider wants to, and maybe even go where the rider does not want to go. Perhaps you know someone who was riding a horse and the horse suddenly turned and went home, even though the person did not want to go there. This happens because the horse decides the rider is not the boss, so the horse becomes the boss.

Remember this; horses usually only want to take care of themselves. If they decide it is better to eat hay at the barn than go for a trail ride, and if they know the rider cannot stop them, they will go to the barn or anywhere else they want to go. Some people say we are not smart. I say that anyone who believes that has never studied us very well. So who is smart? Remember that we respond well to humans who understand us and show they know how to handle us.

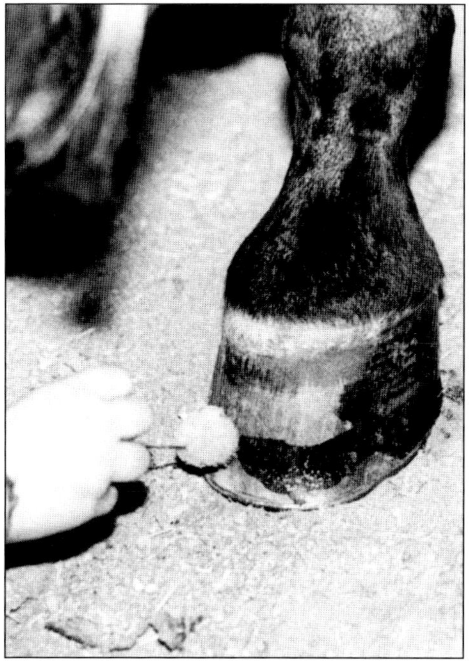

Remember that we respond well to humans who understand us and show they know how to handle us.

Now that you understand more about our behavior, you should be very careful when working around us. Horse trainers work with horses to make sure we are safe for humans to ride and work around. But never take that for granted. Remember, we can get scared easily and accidentally step on you. You should always talk to us when you approach and let us know you are there. Never walk up behind a horse, because he could kick you if you frighten him. We can sense your emotions and can manipulate the way you perceive us.

Before you work around us, make sure you have a professional trainer teach you about how to handle us. Always remember we want you to understand us and treat us with respect. This can help make us both happy as we go along together.

☑ ***Good Job!*** *Go to the back of the book and check the completion box for the* **Behavior Chapter**

Photo by Reg Batt and Herb Stokes

Many Happy Trails to You!

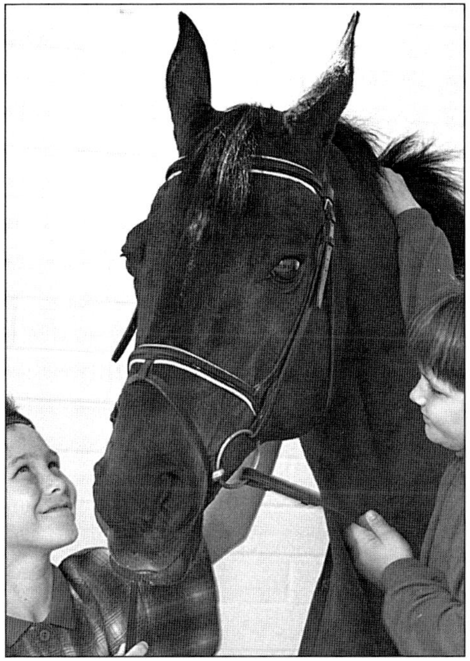

Photo by Reg Batt and Herb Stokes

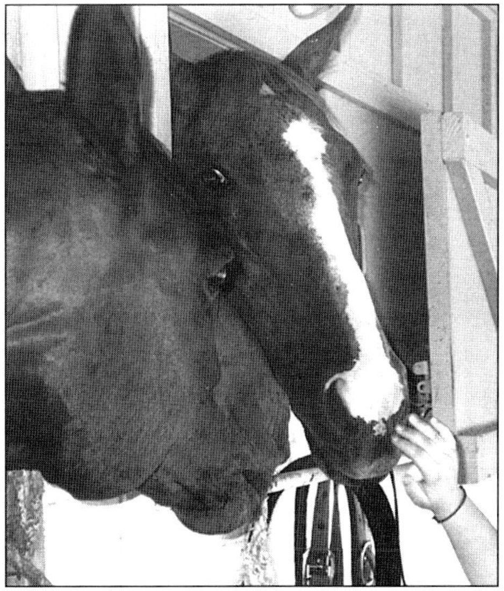

As this book comes to a close, I truly hope you have enjoyed our time together, and have learned some things about horses you never knew before. I would like for you to keep on learning about horses as you get older, and I can promise that there is much more to learn than what I have talked about here.

I believe that the more you learn about horses, the more you will want to know about them. The more you want to know, the better the chance is that you will know at least one horse very well. It is through this type of relationship that you will find a friendship like none other you have ever known, and perhaps even give you a happier outlook on life. Imagine what it is like to have a horse who likes you so much that when he or she sees you they greet you with a nicker to say "hello". Then when you get close enough they want to put their nose softly to your cheek, and make you know that they are happy you came. For many people, the only reason

Photo by Mary Phelps

they have a horse is to experience this friendly bond. Other people have said that due to a relationship with horses, they were able to learn that all living plants and animals depend upon each other, and that humans are the ones responsible for ensuring we are all well cared for.

To make this friendship safe for both of you, you need to keep learning about how horses think and act, and how to care for them. For example, when you work closely with a horse you must always think about how the horse may react to something you do. Most horses like it if you are quiet and do not move quickly or jump around when you are near them, which could cause them to be frightened. They do not want you to do things which may hurt them either, and almost all of them want you to do special things just for them, like give them a treat when they do something well for you.

I bet you know many people who are the same way. If you frighten or hurt someone, they will react to what you have done. If you are careful to consider how another person feels or how you can cause them to be happy, they will react in a completely different way. You also know from reading this book that all horses are not alike, and one horse may act very different than another. This is also true of people.

One big difference between humans you know and horses is that we depend on you to take care of us. In order to have healthy, happy lives, we must have a human who cares about us and will make sure we have everything we need. The only way we can have those things is if you give them to us.

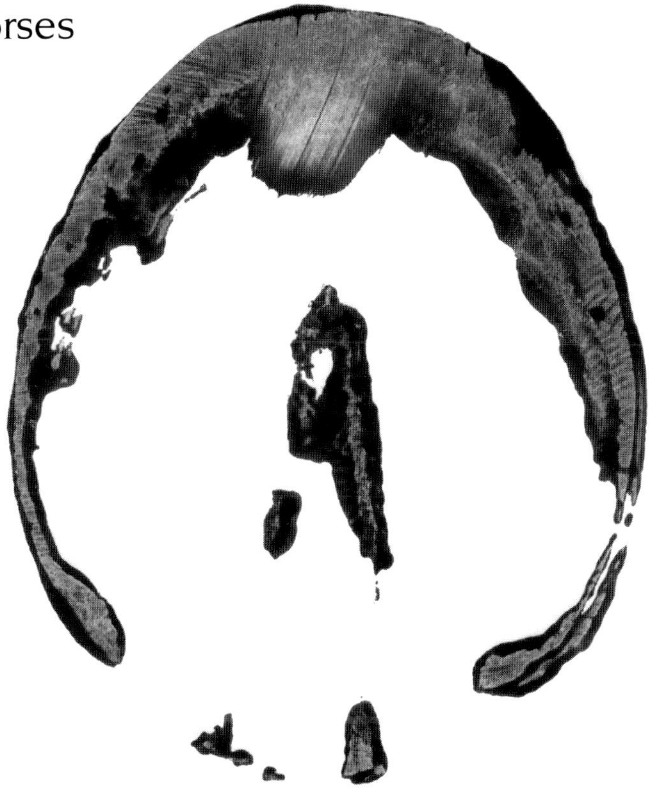

If you care for us, we can give you things also. We can be the best friend you ever had. We can carry you safely for long periods of time and give you a sense of freedom, safety and strength. We can go slow when you want, or very fast. We will work hard for you to repay you for making us happy. We will also be honest with you and let you know if you ask us to do something we do not want to do.

Thank you for spending this time with me. I have enjoyed it very much. Who knows, perhaps we will even meet each other personally sometime and travel happy trails together.

Love,

Champs

Good Job! *Go to the back of the book and check the completion box for the* **Many Happy Trails to You! Chapter**

To Parents
and other Significant Adults

Ask children less than ten years old what their favorite animal is and the answer will most often be "a horse". Many children hold horses in such high esteem that they seem mesmerized when in a horse's presence. For those lucky enough to truly know a horse, the attachment gets only stronger.

For these youngsters, horses are magical beings. They can give children freedom to experiment and go fast without having a driver's license and their parents' consent. They are "dear diaries" for many, since children can spill their feelings to a horse with no fear of being made fun of or having a sibling get hold of it!

A relationship with horses can also foster traits of nurturing and love in children. This is especially true when the child engages in a daily ritual of feeding and caring for a horse. Horses have also been known to make the most unhappy child feel good again, and learning to ride is almost always a sure way to build confidence and enhance self esteem for children.

A true devotee to horses may tell you that the best sensation in the world is to have a horse accept you as one of its own. To have them rub you with their muzzle and smell your face just as they would another horse. To be accepted and have a horse communicate that fact in a fashion that both parties know that something special just passed is, for some, the ultimate in friendship.

An overwhelmingly important factor in making sure this experience is positive for a child is a supportive adult. Whether that person is a parent, a friend, or someone who simply recognizes the importance of this child/horse relationship and cares enough to participate, adults must be involved. Adults are usually better equipped to make the necessary judgments required to ensure a child's safety, the proper riding environment, the horse's safety and other aspects of situations that require "common sense" (which adults are supposed to have).

As with any other childhood devotion, adults are also necessary for a myriad of common tasks. Transportation, preparation, pep talks, moral support, financial support, sitting through practices and being present for important events are as important with horse occasions as with other sports, music lessons or school plays. In essence, it is the adult who helps ensure that the child's experience leaves them healthier, happier, smarter and more comfortable in dealing with other children, adults, and animals.

Hopefully, all truly interested children will eventually have the chance to own a horse. Here again, adults are critical since this is not an inexpensive project. Feeding, providing riding lessons, shoeing and finding a good vet are things that need to be considered.

Buying, Boarding, Training and Lessons

Following is a brief discussion of these topics. It is intended as a starting point. Armed with the information provided here, a person should proceed with careful consideration and many more questions in this venture.

Just as in buying a car, the actual transaction of buying a horse can be very straightforward. Money and papers change hands and title is transferred. But unlike a car, a horse cannot simply be parked and ignored until a person is ready to use it. Horses are an ongoing project.

Careful planning before buying a horse will help assure much greater enjoyment later. General considerations include matching a child with the right horse, arranging for stabling in an environment that is healthy for the horse and reasonably accessible to the child, and providing riding lessons from the right trainer. The best way to accomplish this is to find someone you can trust to help you. Otherwise, you can quickly be taken advantage of.

A good starting place may be a local stable. Another possibility may be a nearby training facility or barn. Should this be the route you choose, be sure to visit as many as practical and visit them more than once if possible. For the novice parent, the purpose of this is to develop impressions of what constitutes professionalism, and then whom among the professionals can be turned to for help.

Professional stables and barns take good care of their animals. Stalls should be cleaned daily and odors from manure and urine kept to a minimum. Compare fees for boarding and find any hidden costs. For example, while some people take for granted that feed is included in the cost, it is not impossible to find barns which do not include feed in their basic price structure. Other possible hidden costs could be things like cleaning stalls, blanketing charges, and laundry charges.

If you are planning to arrange for riding lessons, similar judgments must also be made.

Question what can be expected on a training bill. Is there a disclosure policy that all costs are identified and discussed before they are incurred? The last thing anyone wants is a surprise involving a horse, a child, and a bill.

In essence, comparison shopping is as important in this venture as any other. In addition to comparing price, you also are comparing conditions in which horse and child will be spending their time.

Because instructors, or trainers, are usually associated with only one barn, this adds another dimension to the search. You may even decide to choose a less than ideal barn in order to get the best training for horse and child. For the novice child, it is very important to find an instructor who is kind, thoughtful, and concerned about the safety of the child and horse. While there are many competent instructors, it is very important to find one who will nurture the child's self esteem, not destroy it.

Visit the instructional area and observe how an instructor handles himself and situations. Consider whether this person is one from whom you would like to take lessons. Does he or she use a professional approach in relating to others? Can he or she identify the basic skills your child should learn, and can you measure the outcomes? What goals would he or she set for your child? Are there other students who this instructor has worked with who have attained these goals? Does he or she start on time, giving value for the money paid? Does he or she communicate well with children and adults? Failure in this area will surely lead to negative emotions and grief.

Here again, a comparison of fees for instruction is an important detail. Remember, also, if something sounds too good to be true, it probably is. For example, a promise to have a child who has never ridden before winning horse shows in three easy lessons is undoubtedly a hoax.

Another important issue is preparation for a child's progression. If you accept that most people who coach Little League baseball are not suited to coach at a professional level, it follows that the right instructor for a beginning rider may also be outgrown. This is natural progression and should be discussed. In essence, the information you are seeking is how far an instructor is qualified to take a rider, and whether that instructor will help find the next trainer if the child decides to advance.

Finally, be sure to consider known organizations that can provide a wealth of information, and which may be the end point of your search. Two of the most readily identifiable are the U.S. Pony Club and the 4-H Club. These types of organizations usually offer quality training and social opportunities as well. For some beginning riders these organizations are the extent of their experience. For others, they are just the starting point. For others yet, they are not a suitable option, depending upon many variables. The organizations are well worth exploring in any case.

It may also be possible to participate as a horse enthusiast without actually owning a horse. It is not unheard of to arrange a lease, or ride a trainer's horse which has been designated the role of carrying beginning riders. However, to progress in skill, horse ownership will probably be necessary.

It cannot be stressed too much that purchasing a horse is a "buyer beware" event. This is not intended to frighten or intimidate the novice. It is meant to offer necessary guidance that will allow the first time buyer to proceed with knowledge and confidence.

Following is an excerpt of a humorous essay and a humorous poem which may help illustrate this. These are by veterinarian, and cowboy poet and humorist, Baxter Black. Read, enjoy, and remember the message as you proceed in this venture.

Tradin' Horses

Horse traders are an uncommon lot. Matter of fact, to be a good horse trader you have to be born with the ability. It's a congenital defect. Sort of a cross between a Ginzu steak knife salesman and a pickpocket.

They have the cunning of a coyote, the shrewdness of an order buyer, the memory of an IRS computer and the conscience of a flat rock.

They place very little value on fancy horse barns, matching truck and trailers, white fences, expensive saddles or two party checks. They get no thrill from owning a good horse. They're only good for one thing. . . to trade. The thrill is in the deal.

Uncle Albert was a horse trader. He never had a good horse. If he did, he never had it for long. He'd sell it. He always maintained a used horse lot. And like any smooth operator, he had just what you needed. He could make the lame walk (for a couple hours), the bad actors tame ('til the tranquilizer wore off), and the old, young again. "You want papers? It'll take a week. You want a palomino? Come back tomorrow."

Uncle Albert never did it for the money. He did it for the fun. For the pure simple joy of wheelin' and dealin'. Now before you get the idea Uncle Albert was unethical, you should understand the rules of horse tradin'. . . there aren't any! May the best man win and the other git skinned!...

The Horse Trader

Have I got a deal for you. Got this horse on a trade.
He don't squint half as bad ridin' him in the shade.

I know he limps a little. Yer eyeball is astute.
But fair is fair, my friend, so I'll throw in a case of Bute.

No! He ain't got the heaves! Though I know he looks the part.
He's just a heavy breather, but he's got a lot of heart.

Bloodlines? Talkin' royal blue. A genuine contender.
I'll have these papers printed; fit any race you enter.

The would-be buyer of this horse just stared and shook his head.
He looked the trainer in the eye and said it when he said,

"The only people *that* I know who'd ride that horse, I'd vow
Are too poor to ride a quarter horse n' too proud to ride a cow!"

Resources and Professional Organizations

Following is a list of informational resources and professional organizations. Most of the organizations herein have complete membership information packets available upon request which outline benefits, dues, etc. These organizations are also resources for current event information through their magazines and newsletters. This listing is for the personal benefit of the reader only, and does not include all possible information sources, riding organizations or horse breed associations. Further, no claims are made regarding the reliability, accuracy, or dependability of information of any group listed here.

The United States Pony Clubs, Inc.
4071 Iron Works Pike
Lexington, KY 40511-8462
telephone (606) 254-PONY (7669)
fax (606) 233-4652

4-H Club
Contact your local cooperative extension office, usually listed in state government section of your telephone book.

North American Riding for the Handicapped Association, Inc.
PO Box 33150
Denver, CO 80233
telephone 1(800) 369-7433
fax (303) 252-4610

United States Dressage Federation, Inc.
PO Box 6669
Lincoln, NE 68506-0669
telephone (402) 434-8550
fax (402) 434-8570

American Horse Shows Association, Inc.
220 East 42nd Street
New York, NY 10017-5876
telephone (212) 972-2472
fax (212) 983-7286

American Farriers Association
4059 Iron Works Pike
Lexington, KY 40511-8462
telephone (606) 233-7411
fax (606) 231-7862

American Veterinary Medical Association
1931 North Meacham Road
Suite 100
Schaumburg, IL 60173-4360
telephone 1(800) 248-2862

Index

B
Bad manners 17, 52
Biting 53, 56
Body brush 42
Body-clips 40
Bridle 41, 44

C
Cartilage 33
Colic 27
Confined 6
Confinement 11
Curry comb 42

D
Dandy brush 42
Diarrhea 16, 29
Domesticated 11

E
Ears 29, 41-42, 57
Eyes 26, 42, 55-56

F
Farrier 24, 34, 36
Feed 13, 15, 18, 25, 29, 55
Foals 16
Founder 16, 28
Frog 34, 44-45

G
Grain 15-17, 19
Grooming 39-41, 43

H
Hay 13-16, 27, 58
Heaves 29
Herd order 54
Holsteiner 5
Hoof 16, 33-35, 44
Hoof pick 44
Horse trainers 59
Horseshoe nails 35
Horseshoes 44

I
Inflammation 28

K
Kick 27-28, 43, 56, 59
Kicking 53, 56

L
Lame 45
Larvae 30-31
Ligaments 33

M
Mane 42-44
Mane comb 43-44
Manure 29, 31, 44
Mares 16
Monocular vision 56

P
Pasture 6, 11-12, 15-16, 31, 39, 49, 56
Pecking order 54
Pneumonia 16, 29

R
Rider 1-2, 5, 58

Rough coat 29
Rub rag 43

S
Saddle 40, 41
Salt 18, 19
Second heart 34
Shoes 35
Shots 30
Sleep 47-48, 53
Sleep of the body 48
Sleep of the mind 48
Stay apparatus 48
Stomach 11, 27, 29
Sweat scraper 43, 44

T
Tail 27, 42-43, 54
Temperature 26, 30, 40
Tendons 33
Throat latch 44
Thrush 28, 44

U
Unsoundness 35

V
Vet 23-24, 27-29, 30
Veterinarian 17, 30, 36, 45
Vices 52, 53

W
Water 18, 27, 29
Worms 24, 27, 30-31

Completion Verification

Chapter	Completed ✔	Parent's Initials
Saddle Up!	☐	______
Food	☐	______
Health	☐	______
Shoeing	☐	______
Grooming	☐	______
Sleep and Rest	☐	______
Behavior	☐	______
Many Happy Trails!	☐	______

Place a check mark by each chapter title upon completion (including Parent's validation initials). Complete the information below. Then return to Heartland to receive Completion Certificate and Completion Medal in honor of your accomplishment.

Name ______________________

Address ______________________

City ____________ State ___ Zip ______

Telephone # ______________________

(for delivery purposes only)

Age ______________________

Did you have fun with this book? ____

Comments: ______________________

____

Cut this page and return for prompt processing. Do Not Copy. Verification must be on original page.

FOLD HERE

Place
First Class
Postage
Here

Heartland Education Corporation
P.O. Box 61178
Phoenix, AZ 85082-1178

FOLD HERE

I Want My Own Copy!

I have completed the order form below,
and would appreciate your prompt shipment of the items requested.

___ copies of Horse of Course Series; Champs The Schoolmaster, @ $19.95 each . . . . $ __________
☐ I am interested in an ☐ Italian or ☐ French version of *Champs the Schoolmaster*
☐ I would like more information on the work of Baxter Black. . . . . Free
Add $2.00 for each book for shipping and handling . . . . $ __________
SALES TAX: AZ residents please add 7% . . . . $ __________
TOTAL . . . . $ __________

PAYMENT:
Check or Money Order
Credit card: ☐ Visa ☐ Master Card ☐ American Express
Card Number ______________________________
Name on Card ______________________ Exp. Date ___ / ___
Authorized Signature ______________________________

SHIP TO:
Name: ______________________________
Address: ______________________________
City: ______________ State: _____ Zip: ______________
Telephone: (________) ______________________________

FAX ORDERS:
(602) 491-3865

POSTAL ORDERS:

Heartland Education
Corporation
P.O. Box 61178
Phoenix, AZ 85082-1178

FOLD HERE

Place
First Class
Postage
Here

Heartland Education Corporation
P.O. Box 61178
Phoenix, AZ 85082-1178

FOLD HERE

Rider-Shari Patterson,
Photographer-Mary Phelps

Rider- Liz Cline (author),
Photographer- Don O'Connor

"Here I am in my 5th Silver Medal
winning ride with Liz Cline"
Photographer- Sheri Scott

Author- Liz Cline
Photographer- Reg Batt

Rider- Anne Patterson Chamberlain,
Photographer- Mary Phelps

Rider- Teri Hallman,
Photographer- J.D. Farrell